FATHERS

FATHERS

SAM MILLER

JONATHAN CAPE

LONDON

1 3 5 7 9 10 8 6 4 2

Jonathan Cape, an imprint of Vintage Publishing,
20 Vauxhall Bridge Road,
London SW1V 2SA

Jonathan Cape is part of the Penguin Random House group of companies
whose addresses can be found at global.penguinrandomhouse.com

First published in the United Kingdom by Jonathan Cape in 2017

penguin.co.uk/vintage

A CIP catalogue record for this book is available from the British Library

ISBN 9781911214328

Printed and bound in Germany by CPI GmbH, Ulm

Penguin Random House is committed to a sustainable future for
our business, our readers and our planet. This book is made from
Forest Stewardship Council® certified paper.

For my parents

PROLOGUE

On the 24th of September 2014, shortly after eating his customary lunch – hummus on toast, some prawns and a few grapes – my father headed upstairs to his bedroom. Halfway up the first flight, he fell backwards, crashing into a wooden dresser stacked with crockery, and onto the terracotta-tiled floor of the basement of the house in which he had lived for more than half a century. One blue fur-lined slipper remained on the step from which he'd fallen. He died two hours later. I was not there.

My father had been ill for a long time. Very ill, at times. And that, for a hypochondriac, is a most shocking thing. But he had recovered, and I felt able to go away, to return briefly to India, where I had lived for more than a decade – foolishly convinced that my father would be there on my return to London.

He never liked it when I went away, or that I had lived for so many years in what he referred to as 'foreign parts'. He would invariably tell me whenever I left London that the next time I saw him he would be 'in a box'. 'And,' he would always add, 'then you'll be sorry.' I might have interpreted this as an attempt to make me feel guilty, or to induce pity. But to me it had become neither of these things. These words were always delivered with a roguish look upon his face. And they became his circumlocutory way of saying how much he missed me; a piece of repeated nostalgia, a self-quotation; a turn of phrase he always used, and always would use, until the day he died. It was something that I told my friends, as a way of describing my father's uncommon sense of humour – and they didn't always get the joke. For this was gentle teasing on the part of a literary hypochondriac, the same man who had written, a good fifteen years before he actually died, this autobiographical couplet:

No poor soul was ever iller
than Karl Fergus Connor Miller

In fact, I almost was with my father when he died. We had spent many of his last days together. I had returned to stay in the old family home in London six months before his death, the same house in which I had been born, fifty-two years earlier. Soon after I returned, a doctor, a consultant in palliative care, came round to the house and said that he had only weeks to live. He survived that first set of weeks – and she came round again, and said he still had only weeks to live. And, stubborn to the end, once more he proved her prophecy wrong.

I had not returned to London out of some sense of filial guilt or duty, but out of a selfish longing to be with this man who had done so much to shape me, whose jokes became my jokes, who had edited almost every word I had ever written. I would try, and this too may have been selfish on my part, to do all that I could to keep him alive and to do all that I could to make him laugh. And he surprised us all – family, friends and doctors – by emerging from the fog of near-death to shine and sparkle once again; still a sick man, but one who remained entirely and indubitably the person I had known all my life. His wit was undimmed, and so was his capacity for affection.

He died on a Wednesday. I had returned to Delhi on the Tuesday to be reunited with a former girlfriend. He spoke to me on the phone on the morning of his death: sweet, warming words, and then he sang to me, as if he knew he was saying goodbye, and wanted to leave me with a happy final memory. When he fell down those stairs two hours later, my mother called me, and there was nothing I could do – or she, or anyone else. An ambulance came and my father was carried to his room. He never regained consciousness and died with the rest of the family at his bedside. I was there, vicariously, at the end of a phone, listening to small cries of anguish from my mother – unable to be quite sure what was happening.

After he died, my sister spoke to me, and told me he would still be there, his body at least, in his bedroom, when I returned the next morning from India. She knew, I think, how much I wanted to see him; how upset I was by his death, and by my absence at the time of his death. But when I arrived, full of desolate expectation and brimming with unspoken words, his bed lay empty; his room had been tidied, fresh air was sweeping through the open window. He had gone. My father had been taken away, at the insistence of the police. A post-mortem was necessary and so he was locked up in a mortuary cold store, one of many cadavers. I was distraught. On the long and lonely flight back from Delhi, I had prepared many things that I wanted to say to my father.

My brother rang the mortuary on my behalf, and, after some wrangling, they said that I could see my father, but only for five minutes, and there would be a glass window separating us. At first, I said I would go. And then I shivered as I imagined him cold, naked, or covered with a white sheet, laid out on a slab. I chose not to see him in the mortuary.

That weekend, I wrote a short story, a true tale, for myself and for my children. It described and gave context to those last words, words of song, that I would hear from my father, down a phone line to India. It's a brief story about his life and mine that I would later read out at his funeral:

I was not a fussy child. I ate almost everything, I had no interest in clothes, and did not care for special blankets or teddies. But I could not bear having my hair cut. It seemed like the most terrible indignity, an assault on my person and identity. It was an embarrassment almost as bad as being seen naked in public. On one occasion, a short back and sides left me with the humiliation of two large tufts of up-ward-pointing hair. My father tried to cheer me up. I was inconsolable. 'I look like Rufty Tufty,' I exclaimed through my tears, a reference to a long-forgotten cartoon squirrel who starred in road-safety films of the late 1960s.

For many years after, I was known by my father as Rufty Tufty, or Rufty for short. I liked being called Rufty, it was better than his older nickname, Thammy Thixpence, an appellation that teased me gently about my childhood lisp; and the name Rufty would endure until well into my twenties. This summer, as my dad lay sick in bed, he revived his children's old nicknames. I became Rufty again, or Sil, short for Silly, a name my older brother gave to me.

On the morning of the day on which my father would die, I called him from Delhi. And he sang to me down the phone line. It was a version of 'Leezie Lindsay', perhaps his favourite of all Scottish ballads. It has this line in the original: 'My name it is Ronald MacDonald, a chieftain of high degree.' But in my father's version it had become 'My name it is Rufty McTufty, a chieftain of middling degree.' These were the last words I would ever hear from him.

As we waited for the post-mortem results, obituaries and other tributes began to appear. This was a welcome distraction, but it was also disconcerting. Most of what was written was accurate and full of praise. He was described in glowing terms, as the founder of the *London Review of Books*, as the country's 'last man of letters', the 'greatest literary editor of his time', or 'the last of the great Bloomsbury men'. It was more than enough to make a son feel proud; but it was also as if my father had been turned into a cartoon cut-out. There was suddenly less depth, no complexity, no ambiguity. Judgements had been made about the kind of person my father was, and that was that. It all seemed as final as his death. I felt as if my father's memory, as well as his body, had been appropriated.

Eventually, I did see my father again – on the day before his funeral. Once the post-mortem was over, his body was transported to the Fulham Road offices of Chelsea Funeral Directors, just five minutes on foot from my parents' home. My brother agreed to come with me, and so just before eleven o'clock we walked up the Fulham Road bearing two poetry anthologies, and were ushered into a small windowless room by a man with a sombre face and a black tie.

Inside were two chairs, and a large beige coffin made of pine, in which my father lay, trussed and coddled in yellow silk, his flaxen hair neatly combed, his lips tightly closed. Here he was, finally, in that godforsaken box of his, just as he'd promised. He was slightly battered about the head from his fall, and, I presumed, because of the post-mortem. His skin had a waxy, mottled hue, and he was wearing his own clothes, supplied by my mother to the undertaker. His eyes were shut, and he looked as if he hadn't eaten for more than a week, which, of course, he hadn't. Here, finally, I broke down, and cried. And then, after a minute or two, once the sobs had begun to subside, I declared out loud, as if I could briefly restore him to life, and as if I was addressing a convocation, that this was to be the final meeting of 'The Shitehawks'.

For many months now, my father, my brother and I had met at eleven o'clock each morning at his bedside. These were meetings of what came to be known as the 'Honourable Society of Shitehawks', a semi-exclusive club devoted to hypochondria, jokes, coffee-drinking, biscuit-eating and poetry. Dad had, at one point during these sessions, before they had a name, referred to himself as a 'shitehawk' – a word of Scottish extraction, he informed us – in an attempt to suggest he was of little worth these days. And we proud sons declared that if he was a shitehawk, then so were we. The Shitehawks were born, with my father as presiding officer – the Chief Shitehawk. Occasionally, others would join in our sessions, my mother, my sister, a grandchild – but they'd usually be driven out by the arcane and often ribald humour, the gentle teasing, the general shitehawkery (as it became known in the family), or the long readings of Scottish poetry which my father so enjoyed.

And so, in the undertakers' parlour, after my brief tearful introduction, the valedictory meeting of 'The Shitehawks' got underway. My brother sketched, drawing our father in his coffin, while I read out some of the poetry he loved so much in his last months, often Scottish ballads that he'd known as a child. 'Leezie Lindsay' and 'Tam O' Shanter' were always the most popular items on the Shitehawk agenda. He adored the poetry of Robert Burns, and 'Tam' in particular, for its mixture of the high-flown and the guttural, the drunken and the magical. I remembered him describing it, many years earlier, as a phantasmagorical poem, and having to look the word up in a dictionary.

And so I read 'Tam O' Shanter' out loud to him once more, theatrically over-performing the lines he loved most, the lines that always made him smile, as if I might be able to make him smile one last time.

> She tauld thee well thou was a skellum,
> A bletherin', blustering drunken blellum;

And as I read these words to my unmoving father-in-a-coffin, I recalled how he would gloss the Scotticisms for me – explaining that a 'skellum' was a good-for-nothing, and a 'blellum' was a babbler. He'd occasionally correct my pronunciation, too, or take – even snatch – the book from me to read a few lines. 'Not this time,' I said to myself, as if I was only just beginning to accept the terminal implications of his death.

I took a deep breath of lemon-freshener-scented air, and continued reading Tam, who was by now riding his horse, Maggie, through what seemed to be an outpost of Hell. I cantered through the next part of the poem and then slowed and stumbled over the two hardest lines:

> Coffins stood round like open presses,
> That shaw'd the dead in their last dresses;

By this time Tam has seen the devil, 'auld Nick, in shape o' beast', and is only saved by brave Maggie, who leads him to safety, but in doing so loses her tail to the grasping hands of a witch. It is a poem that warns against and revels in the pleasures of drink and of the flesh, and if anything could have raised my father from the dead, then this was it. I tried to will him to move: a blink of an eyelid, an unpursing of his lips, a slight finger spasm, the tightening of a neck ligament. But my imagination could not get the better of me. He did not flinch, even in my mind's eye. My brother looked up at me from his sketchbook, as if to enquire silently what I might do next.

I plunged on with my next reading, a poem my father had introduced me to as a child: 'Not Waving But Drowning' by Stevie Smith. He had shown me, as a six-year-old, a book he had edited about new writing in England. I flicked through its pages, and put it down, disappointed. 'There are no pictures,' I said, mournfully. He picked it up and read to me this poem, and then I read it back to him. I did not understand it then, but I loved its sadness and its rhythms. I learned it by heart and performed it on stage at primary school. I still do not quite understand the poem, but as I sat beside my father in his coffin, its opening lines seemed to have some oracular meaning, as if I wasn't trying hard enough to communicate with him.

> Nobody heard him, the dead man,
> But still he lay moaning

Finally, I spoke the words of Leezie Lindsay to my father's corpse, with the alternative wording that he had sung to me a few hours before he died: 'My name it is Rufty McTufty, a chieftain of middling degree.' And then I stopped, and looked at my brother. I did not need to say anything to him. He knew I wanted to have my last moments alone with Karl Miller.

My brother left the room. I was alone with my father. I stood up to look more closely at him. But I could not bring myself to kiss or touch his skin, for fear that it would feel like something else, and steal from me my memory of that final kiss of each of his cheeks, back in his bedroom in Limerston Street. And then, standing, shifting my weight from leg to leg, I began my final speech to him, a peroration honed on the flight back to London, practised over and over again in my head and now delivered through hiccoughs of grief.

First, I apologised for crying and for being so sentimental. He would always write a big 'W' in black ink in the margin of anything I wrote that was a little too winsome – knowing full well that he could be just as winsome as I; and I reminded him of that. And then it all came pouring out. I said things to my father, or to his bodily form, that I could not say in front of others, or whilst he was alive – things that I had waited to say and wanted to say for many years. For in some important ways, I owed him more than my siblings, more than anyone really. I spoke of family secrets, of a friend of his who had died many years earlier, and I spoke of gratitude and grief, and, most of all, of love.

PART ONE

I

It is now more than a year since my father died.

On the anniversary of his death, fourteen of us, family and a few friends, made our way to the Pentland Hills outside Edinburgh. We stood at the edge of a forest of Scots pine in the pouring rain and dipped our fingers into a large maroon box provided by Chelsea Funeral Directors. We each threw handfuls of ashes, well-powdered and beige, into the wind, and watched silently as Karl Miller's remains were carried through the damp air like swirling Scottish mist.

But I kept, secretly I think, a small portion of his ashes. And they are with me still, in the inside pocket of the raincoat I wore in the Pentlands. The other day, after going to dinner with some BBC colleagues in Tunisia, I reached into that pocket, searching as usual in the wrong place for my mobile phone. And out came my fingers, marked to the first joint by a beige-coloured dust. A colleague looked at me questioningly. I said nothing, and blew my father's ashes from my fingers onto the backstreets of Tunis.

In the days after my father's funeral, I announced to myself that I wished to try to make some kind of sense of his life and death. I began to write about him, and also about his friend Tony White, and my mother and me. But I did not do this in the expectation of uncovering a hidden truth, or an objective reality that had eluded me until then. Something close to the opposite, really. I think it was actually an attempt to make me feel better; a way for me to deal with grief and guilt. I like to write, you see, and in writing I can console myself. And I want to write before I forget. So I have been writing my version, and mine alone, of the life of Karl Miller.

3

My father always liked to describe himself as an orphan.

He did this in a way that suggested being an orphan was the most important fact of his childhood, though not one that should necessarily evoke pity. It marked him out, as a child, from other people he knew. It was a defining feature – and he would argue later, in a memoir that he wrote when he was a grandfather, that it would help explain something important about his character: what he saw as his divided self, his multiple personality.

'An orphan self took hold,' he wrote, 'vulnerable and fierce, bereaved and aggrieved. It came and it went; in time it was tempered and concealed, rather than outgrown.'

My father was an orphan in the sense that he never lived with either of his parents, who separated before he was born. And he had no siblings. His mother was, undoubtedly, present at his birth in August 1931 in the village of Straiton, outside Edinburgh – but headed off on her own soon after. He did not know if he had been breastfed, and never thought to ask. He was handed to the care of his mother's mother, my father's adored granny, Georgina. They remained in Straiton for his first two years.

My father liked to tell the story that insignificant little Straiton was so named because it was 'straight on' to Penicuik; though I remember being disconcerted on noticing that, when recounting this tale to someone who might not have heard of Penicuik, he would change the destination to Edinburgh.

I wasn't always entirely convinced by my father's stories, which he occasionally exaggerated and which sometimes metamorphosed into what he referred to as jokes, and which I think of also as teases. 'Thammy Thixpence' was one such joke at my expense, and as a child I was once heard to cry out loud, 'I wish there weren't such things as jokes.' He never let me forget that, particularly when I became a teller of jokes, sometimes at his expense. I suppose I objected to being teased, and later learned how to tease back.

I was, as you may have guessed, a pedantic and solemn child, who once suggested to my father, in a forthright manner, that he wasn't a real orphan – like Cinderella, or Mowgli, or Oliver Twist – because his parents hadn't been dead. I don't remember his precise answer, except that he seemed to take pleasure in my orphan repartee, and suggested somehow that orphans might come in many shapes and sizes. He felt orphaned, in spite of the love of his grandmother, and that stayed with him. He never, for one moment, made me feel orphaned.

5

My father didn't have any first cousins that he knew of, though his aunt Jessie had a stillborn child. This child's churchyard burial, in the smallest of coffins, was one of his early memories, but not quite the earliest.

6

At the age of two, my father was moved to the mining village of Gilmerton, even closer to Edinburgh than Straiton, where his first act was to taste a laburnum leaf. This bitter moment became his earliest memory. He lived there until adulthood, sharing a two-bedroom bungalow with his grandmother, two maiden aunts called Peggy and Betty – and Uncle Tommy, with whom he shared a bed, and whom my father liked to describe as 'a simple soul'.

7

My father's parents were always said to have been able to agree on just one thing: their son's name, Karl – with its unusual (in Scotland, at least) initial 'K'. His mother considered herself a good Communist, and saw her son's name as a tribute to Marx, while his father had been a prisoner during the First World War and had made friends with a German farmer called Karl.

His parents remained something of an enigma to my father, both of them leading rather sad, solitary lives – never formally separating, nor finding other partners. He imagined their courtship as a love story and never quite understood what went wrong between them. It was the Great Depression – a time of mass unemployment in Scotland – and my father thought there may have been an argument about what kind of job his father might do, especially now there would be a baby to support, and that he may therefore have been the cause of their separation.

My father wrote that he had 'never been conscious of bearing my parents any ill-will for not being around', though he left open the question of how his abandonment might have affected him in other ways. He could not remember ever embracing or being embraced by either of his parents (though he described how much he loved kissing his granny's cheeks and pulling her earlobes – and he became an indefatigable puller of earlobes in adult life). He talked of his parents' 'failure to remain married to each other, or to me', as if to remind and reassure himself that the fault cannot really have been with him.

He was deeply interested in his parents, both for themselves, and for what they might help him understand in himself. And his father came under particular scrutiny, as a potential role model for someone whose life would take a very different course.

For me, his son, this is a matter of consequence. I want to understand, for reasons that will become clear, what being a parent, and more specifically, a father, meant for Karl Miller.

During his childhood, he saw his mother regularly; his father very rarely.

His mother, known as Minnie, worked as a bookkeeper, an accountant of sorts, mainly in Edinburgh, though in the late 1930s she lived in London. And this London sojourn was the source of one of my father's favourite coincidences. She stayed for a while at number 13 Limerston Street, in what was then a solidly working-class area of Chelsea. And, almost a quarter of a century later, not long before I was born, my father (with my mother and brother) moved into a house in the same street, number 26 – the house where he would see out his days. And Minnie, on hearing of the move to Limerston Street, told her son, 'At last you've moved back among your own people.'

She had previously accused my father, who by this time had been to Cambridge and had worked for both the Civil Service and the BBC, of being a traitor to his class. She had little idea that gentrification was already sweeping the western borderlands of Chelsea in the early 1960s – and would have been astonished that this part of London, where she had once lived, would become in the new millennium one of the most outrageously expensive in the city; a haven for oligarchs.

11

Minnie was famous in her family for her disapproving glances and her withering put-downs. On seeing one of her sisters who visited her in hospital after not speaking to her for many decades, all she could say was, 'You're auffy auld.'

She was also remembered by her only child as saying about that only child: 'Half an hour of him is as much as I can take.' That remark may have been passed on by her estranged husband.

Minnie's real name was Marion, and her sisters' favourite Minnie-joke was to say: 'Marry in haste, repent at leisure.' Read it out loud.

12

As an adult, my father saw much more of his father, William. They both lived in London, and William was a regular visitor to my parents' first home, near Gloucester Road tube station, and then to that house in Limerston Street in which I was born and my father died, fifty-two years apart.

William is best remembered in the family for teaching my brother, as a small child, to dance on graves in the local cemetery. It is not remembered why, but he seems to have had a certain contempt for organised religion, and took a rationalist's delight in testing out superstition.

William showed less of an interest in politics and in class than his estranged wife, though he did sometimes describe himself as an anarchist. He had studied at the Clapham School of Art in London and he continued to paint, obsessively: small, carefully observed Pissarro-like landscapes in rural and urban settings. He never made money from his paintings – and never showed any desire to do so. The ghosts of success and failure seemed not to haunt him; painting was just what he wanted to do. He did have jobs which brought him a small income: at a commercial art studio and sorting telegrams in a post-office. He worked for the fire brigade in the Second World War, and was briefly imprisoned when he went absent without leave on a painting trip to the countryside. But William was, according to his son, always uncomplaining – content with the most frugal of lifestyles, almost friendless and penniless, subsisting on Ryvita and prunes, living in the most austere of London bedsits.

13

I did not know William.

For years, I thought I had a memory of him – a small, wiry, silent old man with a large forehead sitting at the kitchen table opposite my father. The memory must have been stolen from someone else's description, or a long-lost photograph. Only recently did I realise that he died just nine months after I was born, in 1962, probably by his own hand.

My father had been doing what he loved above all else on the evening that his father's body was found – watching a football match. A tannoy announcement led to his hasty exit from White Hart Lane, where Spurs were playing Wolverhampton Wanderers, and he went straight to the morgue. After the inquest, and before his funeral, William's open coffin was placed in what later would become my childhood bedroom in our family home. There were just five people at his funeral.

I found William Miller's death certificate among my father's papers. He died in a south London flat, poisoned by a gas fire. The inquest returned an open verdict, indicating that it was either an accident or suicide. My father, always intrigued by the act of suicide, weighed up the evidence. He conceded that it was just possible that his father was trying to keep warm, but this was unlikely given his general parsimony and the fact that it was only early September. Karl also pointed out that his father, on an earlier visit to hospital, had taken a knife with him, in case, as he put it, 'the news was bad'.

In the months before his death, William Miller had been ill with emphysema; and my mother invited him to come and live with his son, daughter-in-law and two small grandsons in Limerston Street. This, my mother recently suggested, may have been the final straw for a man who had never showed the slightest desire to live as part of a family.

14

My father chose a very different life from that of his father. And he felt that there was a deliberate choice involved – as if he might have decided, in his own words, to become 'a tramp or a monk', both plausible descriptions of William Miller.

He wrote about how he gave a lot of thought to his father's way of life and was both 'impressed by it and warned by it', and about how, instead, he decided 'to join in and join up'. He chose employment as a literary editor and as an academic, occupations that were not naturally solitary.

Most of all, Karl was unlike his father in that he wanted his own family, and a home. He wanted children who lived in the same house as him, even, as we would discover, when they were grown up and had children of their own. He adored his grandchildren, and let them know it. He wanted friends – and he had legions of them, until his dying day, who turned up, in their hundreds, for his funeral.

In spite of these gregarious, householder choices he made, my father continued to speak admiringly of the life of his hermit father: 'He did not complain, and he went on with his art to the end. I liked that in him, and I disliked and feared the filial converse in myself – a dependence on others and the opinions of others.' My father chose to enter that world of dependence: the world of success and failure, of connections and fame, of reputation and dissimulation.

Karl Miller became, according to my mother (who pretends not to like jokes, but who has a good line in sly teases) 'a man of destiny'. By this she meant he was one of several confident men of his generation who seemed born to opine and judge, who had progressive views about most things, and who sometimes behaved as if the world had been made with their future success in mind.

15

However, my father never attempted to throw off his past, nor did he show any wish to do so. And his background – a working-class orphan from a Scottish mining village – went unconcealed; it was never an embarrassment. But on the other hand, he did not romanticise poverty, though there were times he may have thought his own more affluent children were just a little spoiled.

He and I once fought on the sitting-room floor, when, as a small child, I claimed an unassigned present at Christmas. The present was a packet of 'Fuzzy-Felt', which had lost the label with my name (and not my sister's, I was certain), which its giver (one of my father's aunts) had undoubtedly placed upon it. He would refer frequently to that tussle, 'the Fuzzy-Felt incident', as one in which he had been worsted by a five-year-old. He had to retire to his study, convinced he was having a heart attack. He was never a fighter, except on the football field.

He would tell us that he had no toys as a child; his only playthings were cotton-reels. Not long before he died I came across a photo of my kilted five-year-old father, blond and sad, standing next to a rather handsome toy plane. 'Ah,' I said, pouncing on the moment, 'so you did have toys – you told us a lie.' 'It was not mine,' he responded promptly with an air

of remembered melancholy, 'it belonged to the photographer; it was a prop. All the boys were photographed with the same plane.'

16

There may have been no toys in his Gilmerton home, but there were books and newspapers, paper and pencils. They were all more than literate. Everyone would read, even simple Tommy.

I remember visiting that house as a child in the early 1970s and watching Tommy sit in an armchair by the kitchen fireside declaiming crime stories from the local newspaper in a voice of appalled astonishment. His growling Edinburgh accent was so thick that I could only work out what he was actually saying by reading the newspaper over his shoulder. He punctuated each story with the word 'terrible', spoken with an emphatically lengthened first vowel, and a trilled 'r'. His sister, my great-aunt Peggy, slaving over the stove, muttered the same word back to him – an act of encouragement and a statement of accord.

17

Just as his father loved painting, my father loved books and magazines. He read and wrote all his life – although for his last six months this became more of a struggle. His final book review was published a week before he died.

My father's earliest surviving text is a postcard to his granny that begins 'Der gani, I hop u ar kep in wel', and there is a more telling note to his mother written soon after, in a similar pre-modern style, and which touches on his early bibliophilia: 'Will you sed me a bok for I wont wun'.

Then came the first of his many magazines, composed in pencil, with four columns of text, a newspaper-style headline, and a drawing of a gunfight in the middle of the front page. 'Getaman' stars the first of my father's many alter egos, Jack Miller, who has a very slow start to his day, rubbing his eyes and eating his breakfast, before going outside to help catch a highwayman. 'More next week,' his eager readers are promised.

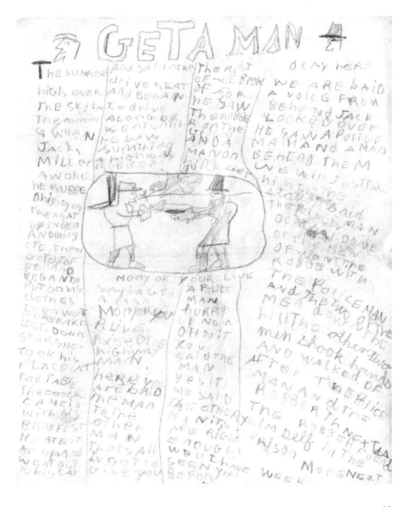

My father was not normally a man of lists. But he did, in recent times, write a long list in his diary, before visiting the doctor, which had the heading 'Woes'. He told me he didn't want to forget what was wrong with him.

In his early teens, he compiled another even longer list. He wrote down every book he read, many hundreds of them, in his journal. And he gave them marks out of 100. *Hamlet* came top, receiving 95 marks; *The Turn of the Screw* lingered at the bottom with a miserly 65. D.H. Lawrence (*Sons and Lovers* – 86) and Aldous Huxley (*Point Counter Point* – 85) were his favourite modern writers, and he described Huxley, to his later embarrassment, as 'the God of literature'. Also embarrassing to him later was a poetry anthology with its teen-age marginalia, which I found on his bookshelves. Wilfred Owen's 'Anthem for a Doomed Youth' is simply 'grand', while 'Hassan's Serenade' by James Elroy Flecker is 'a delicate, colourfully drawn cameo', and Edgar Allan Poe's 'To Helen' is described as a 'surprisingly fine poem'.

My father discussed books with both his evanescent parents. Minnie was a great reader, he recalled, particularly of Proust – whose name she said so that it rhymed with deloused. He did not dare to correct her.

It was William, meanwhile, who had pushed the works of Aldous Huxley in his direction. William also quoted Nietzsche to my father,

'When you go among women, don't forget your whip.' My father thought (or hoped) that this was a joke, or a half-joke, at least. He was amazed to discover that his parents, long estranged, were concurrent readers of Dostoyevsky; maybe they did have more in common than everyone thought.

He later wrote of his surprise at discovering as an adult that 'the working class were not the only ones who read books'. When I tell my friends about my father, I quote that line – because it seems counter-intuitive to many people, and yet it explains for me something important about Karl Miller and the world from which he emerged.

20

My father enjoyed studying, and success came easily. He was quick-witted and had a good memory – and he floated comfortably to the top of the Scottish school system. Indeed his old report cards show that he was top of everything, except Maths. In his mid-teens he told his diary that Maths and girls were his Achilles Heels; he later wrote that they both 'made my temples throb, my pulse quicken, my mouth a lime-kiln'.

He won a scholarship to the venerable Royal High School, eight hundred years old, perched halfway up Edinburgh's Calton Hill, and occupying a wonderfully overwrought neo-Classical building, mod-elled on the Temple of Theseus in Athens. Here he flourished, and encountered, in the person of an inspirational English teacher called Hector MacIver, someone who became his friend and his champion. Apart from simple Tommy, there were few men in my father's early life. There was an uncle who went down the mines, and somehow emerged, decades later, as a successful businessman – but that world was one that never interested my father.

21

Hector gave my father his first sense of how a man might be in a quite other world: the world of literature, of poetry, of Romance and of aesthetic judgement. Hector was a gifted teacher, and the school at which he taught had a long literary tradition of which it was proud. Walter Scott had been a pupil there, and so had a seventeenth-century poet called William Drummond of Hawthornden, with whom my father, for reasons I've struggled to understand, had a special relationship – as if Drummond had been reborn as Karl Miller.

Hector watched over my father's editing of the school magazine, and as he wrote a play that was performed at the Royal High. He took my father out drinking in Edinburgh pubs, introducing this sixteen-year-old to his circle of friends, which included the foremost Scottish poets of the day: Hugh MacDiarmid and Norman MacCaig. 'The thought that we were provincial,' my father later wrote, 'never crossed our minds.'

22

My father, too, took to poetry. He composed teenage verses which would embarrass him in mid-life, but, as he lay dying, brought smiles of nostalgia to his face. Many of these were good poems. Dylan

Thomas, who was a friend of Hector's, wrote warmly of them. But for reasons that my father was never quite able to explain he stopped writing serious poetry.

It was something I pushed him on in those final months, simply because the poems, all published in his school magazine, seemed so confident and mature. He didn't really know the answer. He suggested that he may have felt he would never be good enough, that he was too derivative, but also that in some existential way he didn't want to *be* a poet. He had another life, or lives, in mind. And so instead he became the champion and early publisher of poets he admired: among them Thom Gunn, Ted Hughes and Seamus Heaney.

23

After my father died, I came across a letter he wrote to his Edinburgh friend Rob Taubman as a nineteen-year-old. In it he hints, in almost immaculate prose, at why he stopped writing poetry:

> Sometimes I think there's no more poems in me. Ideas for poems are worth ten times the thoughts they are made of. It's the line, the rhyme, the flesh that counts, not the holy ghost. It's the thoroughly maculate conception that counts.

I love those precocious teenage sentences, and the way they spill out of each other, and play around with Christian metaphor. They almost seem, in their poetic flesh, to contradict what my father is trying to say. Read them again.

In 1947, my sixteen-year-old father got a job at the first Edinburgh Festival as an extra in an opera: a visiting production of Verdi's *Macbeth*. He carried a torch. Backstage, he made friends with Ernest Berk – an Anglo-German dancer and choreographer – and soon met his wife, Lotte. The Berks had moved to England as refugees from Nazi Germany with their daughter Esther. They became his new best friends. He would make one of his earliest forays out of Scotland to stay with them in London, in a building called The Grampians in Shepherd's Bush. The Berks – husband, wife and daughter – gave him his first prolonged exposure to what might be considered the traditional family unit.

But the Berks were far from traditional. They would eat when they were hungry, rather than at mealtimes. Sexuality was openly discussed – as was modern ballet. Clothes were discouraged at The Grampians, particularly by Ernest who was an evangelical nudist, and who used to tease my father about his bashfulness.

On the only occasion my father felt courageous enough to emerge naked from his bedroom everyone else was fully dressed. He made his excuses, and ran back inside. My father enjoyed telling us children this story, and we loved it even more – especially in those teenage days when the prospect of being naked in public seemed to represent a fate worse than death.

His friendship with the Berks was more important than he used to let on. They introduced him to the avant-garde, they provided him with a home in London – and Lotte, eighteen years older than my father, would become his first lover.

In early March 2014, I went back to London for a short holiday. My father's health had worsened. I had just launched my new book in Delhi, the last my father would ever edit, and I felt that I had failed, in my bookish excitement, to keep track of what was happening to him. I hadn't realised from my phone and email conversations with my mother and my siblings how bad things had become, or perhaps they hadn't quite realised themselves – his condition deteriorating imperceptibly each day.

I had not seen my father for more than two months – and the contrast with my previous visit was shocking. He slept most of the day, and would not come downstairs. He struggled to make it to the bathroom, and could not read or sustain a conversation for more than a minute. He barely ate. He was gaunt, dull-eyed and there was no flesh to his sunken cheeks; his stomach was concave. I could see the outline of his pacemaker through the skin of his chest, his ribs jutted out, like plastic cutlery covered by a bedsheet. He forced himself to smile at me, briefly, and held my hand as he drifted in and out of sleep. He asked no questions, which was so unlike him. He seemed to have given up.

Early one morning matters got still worse. This was the email I wrote at the time to my best beloved.

> 430 AM: I hear someone, a woman's voice, calling out for me in a dream. But of course it is not a dream. It's my mother, and I descend the stairs to my father's room. He's lying on the floor, on his side, curled up like a sleep-

ing baby, dressed in a smart blue shirt, surrounded by the objects of his life – his pens and books, and a magnifying glass, and spilled cups of liquid, and medicine packets. His eyes are open. He's unhappy to be there, but not desperate.

My mother is desperate, she says she just found him like that, and he can't move, and doesn't know how he came to be there. I'm able to help him gently into a sitting position, and he then tries to climb back into bed. But he can't really get up. And for half an hour he is on his knees, leaning over the bed, rigid, unable to move. Several times I try to lift him by his armpits but this causes him pain and he gets upset with me. My mother and I think it is better if he can do it himself. But he can't. And so eventually I do lift him onto the bed. And he looks at me with anger and fear, and says that was 'cruel', and that I was torturing him. He calls me an 'assassin'. He has never spoken to me like that in his life. My mother keeps reassuring me, telling me that he doesn't mean it, telling my father that I was such a help.

And I return to my bed, and try to get back to sleep. And I lie there and I remember how when I was a child I used to watch football with him on TV on Saturday nights. I would sit on his knee and fall asleep (I was never very interested in football), and he would carry me to my bed, and I would be in that strange happy border-land between sleep and wake. And so I lay there in my bed thinking of all this, and suddenly I began to sob. And as the sobs subsided I got out of bed and decided to write an email. This email. And now I will try to go back to sleep.

I woke later to hear a district nurse talk of moving my father to a hospice; a very nice place, she insisted, not far away – in London, close, I discovered later, to where his father lived and died. I spoke to the district nurse. My mother, she said, was finding it hard to cope. It would be better for him and for her if my father went into a hospice, just for a few days.

Later that day, on a solitary wander through the city of my birth, I decided it was time for me to leave my home in India. None of us wanted him to go to a hospice. He would hate that most of all. I could not even bear the idea of raising the subject with him. I decided I would be with my father as long I was needed. Until his death, I thought to myself.

25

In April 1948, my father's grandmother died. He was not with her.

In his diary, he wrote, 'The person whom I loved most in all the world is dead.' He'd been having, he later told me, mournfully, 'a merry old time', visiting the Berks in London. And he minded terribly that he hadn't been there, and that he hadn't been told by his aunts how ill she was. His grandmother had, apparently, told them, 'Illness fricts him. Let him enjoy himself while he is still young.'

But my father felt as if he had been punished for enjoying himself (as I would when he died sixty-six years later). And now his anchor had gone. There was even talk of him staying with one or other of his parents, but he remained in Gilmerton with his aunts (and Tommy) and finished his schooling.

26

He was fond of these aunts, particularly Peggy, five foot nothing, and the flintiest of them all – but she did not fill the gap left by his grand-mother. Peggy was a dressmaker who worked from home and became the head of the household – someone whom I would know and love as a child.

She had a sternness to her that was all show by the time of my appearance, but was sometimes a little too real for my father. Peggy and her younger sister – flighty, ditzy Betty – were not very kind about my father's parents, and my father felt this as a burden on him.

'They treat me like an outcast,' he wrote in his diary. 'I shall break out soon.' Peggy read this diary, also full of carnal longings and thoughts of suicide, and warned him of what 'was coming to him'. She would have considered this part of her ward's moral education. Fortunately, her Greek was non-existent – or else she would also have learned how often he masturbated.

27

In his memoirs, my father wrote in comic detail of his early fumblings: the 'solemn hand' on 'soft scone breasts'; his 'urchin thrusts' into a small, freshly dug hole in the earth (the earth didn't move); the schoolboy ogling of schoolgirl cleavages; his hand creeping slowly up the thigh of a girl called Sheena, until, short of the summit, it was locked by Sheena's 'escorting hand' in a vice-like grip.

He wrote a poem about masturbation called 'The Wasting Fires', which he describes as 'especially poor' (and which, perhaps fortunately, has not survived). But sexual intercourse, as he liked to call it, did not happen until some time later. And Carnal Miller, as he nicknamed himself, had to wait.

He would have preferred his last year in Edinburgh to be devoted to the arts of lovemaking. But he made the best of the fact that it wasn't, and dedicated himself instead to being – according to his own account – a slightly pleased-with-himself schoolboy hero.

The school magazine, which he edited, even has a poem about him, 'For K.F.C.M', written by a fellow pupil, which refers to the 'straining catchline' of Karl Miller's 'genius', and of his need for 'the staff of love to lean on and to feel your way'. I was able to embarrass him with this poem more than sixty years later, both for its glorification of an editor ('do you know of any other editor who has published a magazine which includes a poem about that self-same editor?' He didn't deign to answer, but looked grandly at me), and for the poem's homoerotic quality.

28

In the same year, my father also had his first modest brush with fame. The Royal High School, with Karl Miller as captain, won the inaugural version of the BBC radio quiz show, *Top of the Form*.

He was befriended by the presenter, Lionel Gamlin, whose ears stuck out like his, and who encouraged his interest in radio and pushed him to choose Cambridge University instead of Edinburgh. He got in to Cambridge, the first Royal High School boy to do so in living memory. He was aglow with success, and the promise of still more.

29

A few months later he wrote to his Aunt Peggy, 'I was a very promising young person last September. What am I now? I am a prisoner.'

Like almost all young men at the time he had been sent away to foreign parts on compulsory national service. His studies were deferred. My father joined, quite absurdly for a man who would never master the art of changing a light bulb, the Royal Engineers. It was soon decided that he was not officer material; he didn't demur. He was unembarrassed – indeed he liked to tell the story – that in an army intelligence test he scored nought out of twenty for reassembling a bicycle pump. My father remained gloriously and happily impractical all his life.

30

He had what he thought was a nightmarish beginning to National Service. He spent many hours peeling potatoes and square-bashing. He was bullied. He was made to lift huge bags of flour, and felt he would disappear into the ground beneath their weight. And, worst of all, there were the long dormitories full of men 'displaying and discussing their erections'. He didn't join in.

He found himself in what he described as the lowest stratum of an eighteenth-century class system. 'The army,' he noted, 'had yet to develop a middle class.' He later wrote that until they joined the army, 'many working-class boys had remained until then remarkably innocent of what it was to be treated like dirt, having at least been spared the boarding-school regime which was thought to have made officer material of the others.'

My father would go on to have many friends who had been to boarding school, and were officer-class, and even had titles, but he never seemed envious or in awe of them. At times, he felt they had missed out on family life even more than he had, as an orphan. And there would never be any question of his own children going to boarding school (or being encouraged to join the army).

My father's National Service nightmare did not last long. There was a minor miracle, as far as he was concerned. He was plucked out of his regiment and sent to Hamburg to join the British Forces Network radio station – a dream job for this particular eighteen-year-old. He never quite understood how he fell on his feet so unexpectedly, but his very small amount of radio experience seems to have come to his rescue. Soon, he was amazed to discover that sneering officers and bullying sergeants had become respectful, even obsequious.

He helped out with the BBC's *Two-Way Family Favourites*, one of the most popular radio programmes of its time. He wrote radio talks about books and films; and his main job, less obviously of interest to him, was as assistant to the head of religious broadcasting.

He travelled across Germany recording church services, and flirting chastely, he insisted, with German girls. There was a visiting English art student whom he liked, but he wrote to his Edinburgh friend, Rob Taubman, that 'she's as cautious, amorously, as a pair of binoculars'.

My father lived in Hamburg's red-light district, and in the evenings he sat at his desk writing book and film reviews, and would stare out of the window, distracted by the prostitutes displaying themselves in shop windows. He told me that he never went inside; though here again was something else I could tease him about. His interest in brothels, I pointed out, dated from his early teens. He liked to tell the story of how he had encountered the word 'brothel' in a book, and he asked his grandmother what it meant. She replied that it was 'a place where bad people go, and dance'.

32

My father may have been unapologetically impractical, but he was surprisingly good with scissors and paste. Several of his ancient scrap albums have survived, including one largely devoted to his time in the army. It is full of wonderfully Romantic images: a Watteau painting of a courting couple on the cover, Dylan Thomas in a bow tie wandering through an overgrown cemetery on page one; further on there's a contemplative André Gide staring at his fingernails – cut out of *Picture Post* – and a still from *Samson and Delilah* showing a bejewelled Hedy Lamarr sitting comfortably on Victor Mature's knee. There are also party invitations, railway passes, a flirtatious telex correspondence with someone called Inge and a Russian-language document that allows Corporal K.F.C. Miller into the Soviet sector.

There's a small advertisement torn from a British newspaper, and sent to him by his father, which found its place of honour in the scrap album. It's about a treatment for blushing and shyness, each of these words underlined by William Miller, with a marginal scribble that says, 'There's hope yet, Karl!!'

His father wrote to him regularly while he was in Hamburg; long, teasing letters – making fun of his Scottishness, his nose, his love of friendship. He also came close to apologising to his only child for having deserted him: 'you have been most unfortunate in the family you were born into – that includes myself, of course.'

33

On visits back to the UK, my father would spend more time with the Berks in London than with his aunts and Tommy in Edinburgh. The Berks had become, in certain complicated ways, a substitute family. He was seen by the two older Berks as an appropriate companion and suitor for their daughter, Esther – and the two were often left alone together. But the most important relationship was with Lotte, with whom he became, as he put it to me, 'more than good friends'.

In his memoirs, he characterised his role in that relationship as being somewhere 'between son and lover'. He goes on to describe how, while he was still a schoolboy, Lotte and he travelled together to Cambridge. He was meeting his future tutor, the pyjama-wearing F.R. Leavis, to discuss the postponement of his studies until he had completed National Service. Lotte sat in a nearby cafe, reading his secret diaries – a love offering of sorts from my father. Later that day their sexual relationship – his first – began. It would continue for the next two years.

In later times, my father was more embarrassed by his diaries than by his relationship with Lotte, about which he talked freely, and in jocular terms – telling me, on several occasions, that Lotte said he had the body of 'a noodle'. He found this both funny and sad, but couldn't quite explain what she meant.

He eventually destroyed those secret diaries that Lotte had been allowed to read in 1949. He used them for his memoirs written in the 1990s, quoting, for example, his third-person account of his own love-making with Lotte: 'He was on her body as a bee moves and edges over a blossom.' But not long after completing his memoirs, he tore every page out of the hardbound notebooks which contained the diaries. The empty covers survive, as a frustrating reminder of something I will never be able to read. I suppose I should not mind – and yet I feel they would have provided me with clues as I sought to unravel my father's complex attitude towards sexual fidelity, and towards what might be seen as conventional monogamous relationships.

Very recently, after my father died, my mother took me aside and told me, apologetically, guiltily, that he had destroyed the diaries after she sneaked a look at them, and had teased him about their contents.

34

A few months before his death, my father and I talked at length about what he christened 'the Lotte ménage'. He told me tales of being taken to an avant-garde ballet performed in Putney and in the nude, of sleeping naked on the roof of The Grampians, of living off potatoes (he imitated the way Lotte barked the word 'Kartoffel' in response to any question about the next meal), and the blind eye which Ernest turned to his wife's sexual adventures.

I searched on the Internet for 'Lotte Berk' and discovered that Esther had written a book about her mother – and herself. It arrived by post two days later. My father flicked through it eagerly and nervously, searching for his name. There were lots of scabrous stories but Karl Miller was unmentioned. He seemed relieved.

I continued, like a battle-hardened journalist, to press him on the subject of Lotte's daughter. In his memoirs, my father quotes a poem of his which he describes as a tribute to Esther:

> This night of nights my smocked and sandalled love
> I saw go through the starlight, while on high
> My limbs grew into knives, I bled my light
> And throbbed my spouting lustres through the sky.

I said to my father that this read like a love poem. He seemed a bit flustered, something that was rare. 'Romantic,' he responded, 'with a capital R.' I suggested that the line about throbbing, spouting lustres sounded almost indecent. He lifted his eyebrows as he always did when he had nothing further to say on a particular subject.

Later, while we sat together in a hospital waiting room, I asked him, straight out, 'so, did you also have an affair with Lotte's daughter?' Just at that moment, the man sitting across from us, whose most distinctive feature was a transparent tube which emerged from his nose and disappeared behind his back, stood up abruptly and moved to another part of the waiting room. My father nodded at the empty chair.

'You can't talk about these things in public.'

'Will you tell me later, then?'

'Yes,' and he smiled, and placed his hand upon mine.

But the moment had passed and we talked no more of Lotte and Esther.

35

After my father's death I found dozens of Lotte's love-letters. And from these it is possible to get some idea of my father's teenage state of mind. Lotte reassures him that he is not ugly. She is upset when he tells her he wishes he were dead, though there is no explanation of why he might have felt this way. Lotte talks a lot about Esther, and it becomes clear that she and Ernest are still thinking of my father as a suitable partner for their daughter.

> I had a long talk with Esther tonight. She felt so sad, because she thought she did not behave very nicely to you and yet she is so very fond of you and so terribly abashed. She wants you to come back soon and hopes a greater and deeper friendship shall become of it. I hope so too of course. But I felt a bit funny – thinking all the time while she spoke that I love you… Is it right? What do you think? Is there a right or wrong in such cases?

I don't know how my father answered these questions, and I would like to. The letters, according to Lotte's descendants, no longer exist.

My guess is that he may have avoided giving a clear answer – as he would some years later, when faced in his own marriage with difficult issues of fidelity and friendship. He had, at this stage in his life, no other married friends except Lotte and Ernest, and no other example of a married couple with a child, except his own parents – estranged since before his birth. Open marriages, one might say, of very different kinds.

36

A few months after my father's death I tracked down Esther Berk, now Esther Fairfax. She remembered my father as a shy, gawky, clever teenager. Her parents were always forcing her and my father together. She remembers a few kisses and fumbles with him, but nothing more. 'He didn't seem very keen on me,' she said. The nudity was very embarrassing. 'Just imagine!'

Her mother told her a few decades later that she and my father had been having an affair. 'She loved him,' Esther told me.

37

My father's closest friend of his late teens was Rob Taubman, almost a decade older than him. Many of their letters survive, discussing girlfriends, suicide and poetry. And they are full of my father's wonderfully, distinctively Karlian sentences, including that girl who was as amorous as a pair of binoculars. Other examples: 'My life is a staggering farrago of irreconcilable experience'; 'What a bag of bones I'd be without my hopes!'; 'I, in my celibate and military fastness, I envy you'; 'It's a great wen of fascination, Berlin.'

38

My father arrived at Downing College, Cambridge in the autumn of 1951.

He would depict himself as an over-enthusiastic ingénu; a fresher who made a fool of himself by wandering about in a college gown, and by painting, in black lacquer, the names of famous poets on a set of white mugs that he'd bought at Woolworths.

He was never à la mode, and he didn't mind. But he made friends easily, and from all kinds of backgrounds, and many of them were modish. Some were friends till the end of his days. Others died early. There's a sad list in his memoirs, written in the early 1990s, in which he refers to his Cambridge friends whom he had already outlived. It begins thus:

> The painter Rory McEwen was to develop cancer. Tony White died of a pulmonary embolism, after a football injury. Nick Tomalin, serving as a war correspondent, was killed by a heat-seeking missile in the Middle East.

39

I stalled for a few moments when I typed the second of those names: Tony White.

It's the earliest of several mentions he receives in my father's memoirs, and he plays an important role in this story. Like my father, Tony became something of a star at Cambridge, the best-known university actor of his generation.

40

My father didn't act, but he certainly did perform. While in his first term in Cambridge, he used to go down to London to host a BBC radio show called 'The Younger Generation', and the notoriety this gave him already marked him out among his college contemporaries.

Varsity magazine devoted a full page to a profile of Karl Miller, headlined 'Northern Light', when he was just twenty years old, and midway through his first year at Cambridge. It's written by Nick Tomalin (the third in my father's list of those who died young) and captures something of that mercurial, oscillatory, fleeting quality that my father noticed in himself.

> His manner is a peculiar blend of shyness and arrogance,
> perception and ingenuousness, tolerance and puritanism; he
> will suddenly switch from the serious to the facetious, often
> bursting out with a surprising flash of laughter or annoyance.
> Many times he will turn from reciting libellous verses about
> his acquaintances to water a sprig of heather he keeps on
> his mantelpiece to remind everyone of his intense Scottish
> patriotism.

41

He gave up the heather, but never those libellous verses. He regaled us with his daft rhyming songs, directed at his friends and foes, until his dying day. Miller, as we have seen, rhymed with iller, and elsewhere might be paired with gorilla or painkiller. Sam could rhyme with damn, or sham or flimflam. And when I went off to the Middle East to study Arabic, I would become, depending on his mood, Sam Mullah or Saddam Miller.

42

My father sent the *Varsity* article to his old schoolteacher, Hector MacIver, who declared it 'damn close to the bone', and forwarded his 'compliments many times over on making yourself already worth writing about'.

43

According to the *Varsity* profile of my father, 'many people are attracted to him by his streak of impulsive gregariousness, and he will make and break friendship with great relish'.

Another early Cambridge friend whom he outlived was the poet Thom Gunn, whose early work he edited and published. Theirs was an intense relationship – a triangle of friendship that included Tony White, and foreshadowed another still more complex triangular relationship.

46

Thom Gunn described getting to know my father in an anthology about Cambridge published in 1977:

> Argumentative, inquisitive, imaginative, he seemed to have no preconceived ideas of what he might find at Cambridge, and he wasn't going to accept anyone else's. His very abrasiveness was part of his charm. And he charmed me off my feet, as he did everyone he didn't irritate…

44

Thom could be abrasive, too. At some point in my father's first year, Thom and my father had some kind of skirmish, and Thom wrote an apologia on an envelope, complete with cartoon drawings, that my father pasted into his scrapbook. 'I behaved very badly last night,' Thom wrote, '[I] must apologise with all my heart for having been so rude, and so reticent. Rudeness is excusable (just), between friends, reticence not… So tomorrow morning I will try and make amends for reticence.'

The three of them, Karl, Thom and Tony, had high expectations of male friendships, as if these would be more enduring and more profound than those that were formed with women. Sometimes, though, these male friendships would be challenged by the sexual preferences of the men involved.

Thom and Tony would remain devoted to each other, but Thom and my father drifted apart. That drift seems to have started when Thom outed himself as a homosexual. My father felt excluded, I think, by this, and by his new all-consuming relationship with a young American student, who became his life partner.

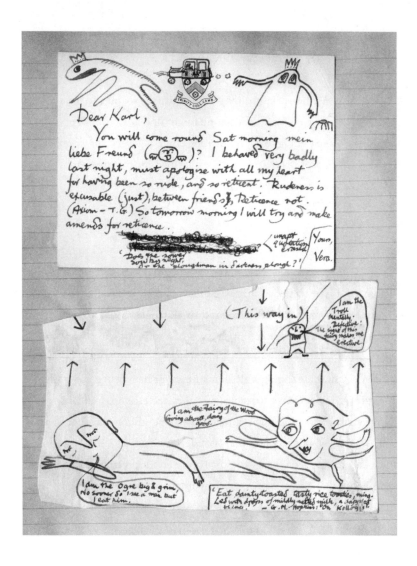

This was something that Tony would later tease my father about, as if Karl Miller struggled to reconcile close male friendship with the possibility or reality of homosexual love. My father was not, I think, a homophobe, but was sensitive to accusations that he might be. And he would sometimes recoil, theatrically, should one refer in any level of detail to the presumed sexual practices of homosexuals. 'Stop it,' he would say, if sodomy were mentioned.

45

My father's Cambridge scrapbooks are a testament to the non-stop sociability of his life at college. He attended large numbers of plays and parties and meetings of literary societies, finding time in between to write short stories, edit magazines and to study. And, eventually, he fell in love. Like Thom Gunn, he met at Cambridge the person who would become his life partner. In his case, it was, fortunately for his children, a woman – Jane Collet – a half-Jewish girl from the Home Counties who was studying Russian and French.

My parents first encountered each other in October 1953, at a party my mother's old school friend Sasha Moorsom (who will appear again in this circuitous tale) gave for her in my mother's first term at Cambridge. Sasha was older than my mother, and was, at the time, for my father, an object of half-requited affection.

My mother remembers thinking that Karl Miller was an interesting man: thin, blond, with very red ears, unintimidating and very Scottish – quite different from most of the people she met in Cambridge.

Some months later, after a visit to the cinema and a Burns Night dinner, they sealed a relationship which lasted, with a few ups and downs, more than sixty years. My father stuck a hotel room receipt in his scrapbook. Mr and Mrs Wood, it seems, stayed at the Cromwell Hotel in Cambridge, on 20 February 1954. Underneath, he wrote 'Our night of love...'

My mother's Cambridge years were very different from my father's. She lived a long way out of the city, in an all-women's college. Women were hugely in demand, she told me the other day. There were so few of them, in comparison. Every day someone or other made a pass at you, or said something about your bum as you walked along King's Parade.

She didn't feel she was special there, since most of the women in her family had been to university, and the clever ones did sciences. My mother didn't love her years at Cambridge, and was rather dismissive of them at the time, but looking back she feels that they had, in obvious ways, a huge influence on the rest of her life. She describes herself as rather empty-headed in those days, with no clear direction or sense of purpose.

She was shocked to read some ancient letters she had written to my father, before they were married: 'I had nothing to say for myself in those days,' she told me. 'I don't know what he saw in me.'

My father loved his time at Cambridge. He could never understand why I, almost forty years later, did not feel the same. It irritated him when I spoke ill of my time there. It was a great adventure to him, full of possibilities, of alternative futures. For me, a middle-class Londoner, it felt crusty and parochial and elitist. I didn't want to be surrounded by people like me – and I was. My father hadn't been surrounded by people like him, and it was at Cambridge that he made his discovery that it wasn't only the working classes who read books. Some of his new best friends were what he referred to as 'toffs'. He was invited to country houses, and met Princess Margaret. He was intrigued by this world, but never quite seduced by it. He also became a member of the secret society known as the Apostles, of legendary and overstated influence, and was befriended by E.M. Forster.

And, in the midst of this social and intellectual whorl, he continued to flourish academically. He got what his friends referred to as 'his First', as if nothing else were a possibility. He stayed on at Cambridge, working towards a PhD, an academic career seemingly guaranteed.

A scholarship then took him to Harvard for further studies – and off he went to the New World for the first time.

48

My father was less happy in America. He wasn't really committed to the subject he had chosen, American Puritans and the Scottish Enlightenment, and was having doubts about academia. At Cambridge he had been an immediate star, while at Harvard he was just another foreign postgraduate and had to work harder to make his mark.

He was lonely too, and delighted when my mother earned enough to pay for the seven-day journey by ship from Liverpool. They got married soon after she arrived.

Both of them later claimed this only happened because their Harvard landlord said that they would not be allowed to share a room. In fact, the marriage had been on the cards for some time.

A few months before he died I came across the primmest of letters that my father wrote to his future parents-in-law, more than a year prior to their marriage. As I read it out to him, he snatched it from me, as if to check the signature – unable to believe he had written something so conventional, and that contradicted the traditional telling of the story of their wedding.

Dear Mr and Mrs Collet,

I am writing to say that Jane and I have been thinking about getting engaged, despite the uncertainty of our futures, and to ask you if you would mind. I'm afraid I'm not very versed in the code of betrothals and hope I'm doing the right thing in writing to you like this. We have also been thinking that there's not much point, as yet, in putting it in the 'Times', though Jonathan, who is my authority in these matters, tells me this should eventually be done. I hope you are both well...

Yours sincerely,
Karl

The aforementioned Jonathan, with whom my father shared a surname, was the boyfriend, and later husband, of my mother's sister Rachel. This other unrelated Miller would soon become well-known for his role in the comedy show, *Beyond the Fringe*, and then, as something of a polymath, was responsible for uncountable operas and plays and TV programmes and books.

51

So my parents' first few months of married life were spent in Massachusetts – but my father soon decided he'd had enough of academic life. He knew there was a Civil Service job waiting for him in the UK, and my parents took a long holiday. They were joined by their old Cambridge friend Rory McEwen (the first in my father's list of those who died young), and his brother Eck, on a journey across America.

The McEwen brothers were in America to sing Scottish folk songs – and my parents were, in the widest sense of the word, their 'roadies'. They remembered that journey in my father's broken-down Buick as a prelapsarian idyll, before children and careers took over their lives.

In those days, my father still liked to travel – and he carefully marked up his road atlas with the dates and distance travelled on each step of that journey from Boston to San Francisco via Texas (where Thom Gunn was living) in the summer of 1956. '6,500 miles according to the speedometer,' he wrote proudly in the margin of the map.

Rory McEwen took my favourite photo of my parents on this journey, dancing at a pit stop, as they drove through the Deep South.

My parents returned to London in the late summer of 1956, and before long moved into a flat near Gloucester Road. My mother was soon pregnant with my brother Daniel, and my father was working for the Treasury, with responsibility for local government funding. He didn't last long there. He was bad at maths, didn't know the difference between rent and rates, and once, in a response to a ministerial query, underestimated the size of the local authority sewage budget by a factor of a million – not forty-five pounds but forty-five million. He left for the BBC, where he was thrown into current affairs television – and he survived there about as long as he did at the Treasury.

He left the BBC because he had been offered what was for him a dream job: literary editor of the *Spectator* magazine. The orphan boy from a Scottish mining village had become an arbiter of London literary taste at the age of twenty-six.

There's something I need to say.

I've been re-reading some of these last little chapters, and I have realised that there's something slightly restrained, even leaden, about them – as if I were just another proud or boastful son telling a series of anecdotes about his recently departed father. It may partly be that a young man making his way in the world is not inherently interesting, or unusual. But I also think it may be because I am withholding some important information for the time being. I've decided that I need to do this, in order to tell the story properly, but it makes me self-conscious as I write. Bear with me.

54

As my father hopped from job to job, he was developing a new obsession: football. With his friend Tony White, he founded Battersea Park football team – a motley group of friends, many from Cambridge, who played every Sunday morning. In those very early days there weren't quite enough of them, and on one occasion my pregnant mother stood in as goalkeeper.

My father had a complicated, addictive relationship with football. He wasn't your average fan, and never really supported a team. Instead, he admired certain players for their elegance and spirit as much as for their match-winning abilities. And he was at his most lyrical when writing about football. He once, in a magazine article, referred to the England player, Paul Gascoigne, as a 'priapic monolith in the Mediterranean sun', and was teased for ever after about this piece of purple prose.

My father had played football as a very young boy in Gilmerton, but not at the rugby-obsessed Royal High School, or at Cambridge. And he showed little interest in football until he moved to London in 1956. Later he wrote that he liked to think that 'by playing football I was rejoining the working class'. He also believed football was in his 'blood', through a grandfather who might have played for Glasgow Rangers, a rare occasion where he suggested that blood might matter.

My father never claimed to be very good on the field, later describing himself as 'a lesser light, and sometimes a darkness' in the Battersea Park team – but he was more than enthusiastic.

Many years later, after Karl Miller had retired and Tony White had died as a result of playing for Battersea, I too became a lesser light in the team these two men had founded.

2014:2

The medical profession gave up on my father late one Friday in March 2014 – on what became known in the family as the 'King Lear evening'.

Occasionally during my father's illness he showed signs of madness. There was a hallucinatory quality to some of these episodes, as if he could no longer distinguish between the world of dreams and of normal consciousness. On one occasion, he fondly and lucidly recalled (to me) how he had spoken warm words at my funeral. On another, he angrily accused my brother and me of being 'patsies': junior parties to a wider conspiracy aimed at keeping some kind of unspecified truth from him. He also sometimes temporarily lost the power to read – he still understood the written word, but went over the same line over and over again, and complained of its repetitiveness.

At first, we, and the doctors, saw this as a sign of some terminal mental decline. But later we came to realise that the cause of these episodes was largely physiological. Urinary infections were turning him batty. Get rid of the infection, and his senses were restored.

My father suffered from two cancers – prostate and bladder – which conspired to make urinary infections de rigueur. These cancers were not moving particularly fast through my father's body; indeed the prostate cancer seemed to have fallen fast asleep since the previous year. However, in March 2014 his bladder cancer seemed to be doggedly making its way up an inner tube towards one of his kidneys. According to his urologist, this tube, the ureter, needed unblocking, and surgical intervention was necessary.

We were told on a Friday morning that a bed would become available at our nearest hospital later that day. We were instructed to report to Accident and Emergency – and a message would be sent ahead to make sure that my father would be spirited from there to a proper bed, and then to an operating theatre. But the staff in the A & E waiting room had no knowledge of his impending arrival.

We sat there for hours, my brother, mother and I each taking it in turns to be with him. And it was then that he failed to answer me about whether he had had an affair with both the Berks, mother and daughter, Lotte and Esther.

As it grew dark, and after several half-hearted attempts by my father to go home, he was pushed in a wheelchair through the mayhem of a Friday-night Accident & Emergency ward into a curtained cubicle. He was beginning to get confused by this time (and so were we all). He mistook the grim-faced tea-lady for a nurse and, gently holding her hand, congratulated her on entering such a noble profession. She seemed pleased by this; her grimness dissipated. She patted my father on the shoulder, and broke what may have been the practice of a lifetime, by giving his two family members – my brother had shown up by now – tea and biscuits.

A nurse did then appear, and took his blood, and measured his heartbeat and his temperature – but she had no idea when a doctor might appear. My father fell asleep, and woke up again almost immediately with a start. He now seemed completely disoriented. And his thin white hair was sticking straight up, as if he had been given an electric shock.

Just then, I heard another Scottish voice that I recognised. It was my father's best friend of recent years, Andy O'Hagan – the latest in a long, long line of close male friends that stretched back to Rob Taubman in the 1940s, and Tony White in the 1950s. Andy appeared, full of honest goodwill and bonhomie – always primed with a few jokes. My father managed to sit up, his hair and arms akimbo, and looked hard at his friend for a few seconds. 'Go away, Andrew,' he commanded, as if he were performing an act of exorcism, or banishing him from the kingdom. Andy, deflated, slunk off; Cordelia, we later decided, had been driven away. We brothers, Goneril and Regan, clung to our father, wondering what would happen next.

Eventually, a doctor came, at about ten in the evening. My father tried to talk to him. He never lost the power of friendly circumlocution, so that he began, 'If you would be so good as to tell me your honest opinion of my condition, I would be...' But he couldn't finish his sentence, and he looked at me as if he'd lost the power of speech. The doctor turned to Goneril and Regan, and told us that our father was not well. We looked at each other with foolish smiles. 'Yes, that's right,' I said, attempting to disguise any note of irony in my voice.

'He's too ill for us to operate. I think you should take him home,' the doctor opined.

I left my brother with the doctors and their discharge notes. And I borrowed a wheelchair to push a raving King Lear, wild of hair and of gesture, through the night-time streets of Chelsea, full of tipsy Friday restaurant-goers. And I'm sure I heard him say, 'I fear I am not in my perfect mind.'

55

I appeared on this earth in January 1962. It had been a complicated conception and gestation, I would later discover. I was also several weeks late, and weighed more, my mother would point out, than the enormous Christmas turkey that she had squeezed into her oven the previous month.

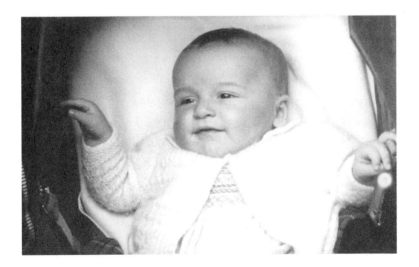

I was born in what is still my mother's bedroom – just after dinner time on a Saturday evening. My mother remembers a full house. My father and some friends, including Tony White, had witnessed the defeat of Fulham at home (three goals to four, I looked it up), by their arch-rivals Chelsea.

Several of them lingered in the kitchen awaiting news of the arrival of the small person who would one day become the writer of these words. My mother later expressed her anxiety that the guests might not have been fed.

56

I was a hungry, solemn child – best remembered for my greed and my humourlessness. I could be tickled or bribed into smiling for a camera, but I seem to have left the impression that I wasn't very keen on the world, or the people who inhabited it.

I have lots of rather dull early memories: of a lizard on a wall during a Spanish holiday; of a boy at playschool whose name actually was 'Boy'; of plucking two leaves from a bush each morning which I gave to my nursery school teacher, Miss Carroll; of becoming furious at being expected to sleep when I wasn't tired.

Only in one of these early memories does my father appear: we were travelling by train, somewhere abroad (Spain, my mother tells me). We were at a station and we had to run for the next connection. My father held my left hand very tight, almost but not quite dragging me along the platform, my legs moving incredibly fast to keep up with the rest of my body – and somehow I managed to remain vaguely vertical. It is a memory that is not entirely reassuring, and yet I do remember, almost as my earliest triumph, that we caught that train.

I never loved football as my father did, and yet it provided an important bond between us until the day he died. We sparred repeatedly on the subject, and I argued against his firmly held football views from, as he frequently pointed out, a position of ignorance.

My son would also become a football aficionado, whose views were greatly respected by my father – and one of my greatest pleasures was watching the two of them arguing about football during the 2014 World Cup, some weeks after my father was supposed to have died, and three months before he ate his final lunch.

Football provided both ritual and a weekend schedule for me as a child. During the week, we were looked after by my mother (who returned from work earlier than my father) and a succession of au pairs. My father emerged at weekends from his world of literary magazines, which kept him working beyond my bedtime on weekdays. I almost always spent Saturday evening and Sunday morning with him. First on Saturday, I would watch *Match of the Day* on television, sitting on my father's knee. It would end late, usually after eleven, and I would invariably fall asleep. When the programme ended, he would carry me to my bed.

Then on Sundays he played football for Battersea Park and he would take me along, whatever the weather, often accompanied by my sister, Georgia, born two years after me. I would stand by the touchline wrapped in hat and gloves while watching them play, and I would go for little wanders – my father keeping a quarter of an eye on me. Once, he told me in more recent times, with one of his teasing glances, I laid the most enormous turd near the touchline, which became an object of wonder for my father and his teammates. Throw-ins, he informed me, became something of a hazard.

My sister and I roamed freely through the changing rooms, while waiting for my dad and his teammates to get showered. We'd remark to each other about how unembarrassed these men were about displaying their willies. Male nudity seemed like the funniest thing, to both of us. My sister pointed out to my father that a red-haired player also had red hair around his willy, and he teased her for decades about her love for the 'red-haired man', a character actor who at one time seemed to appear in every British film and TV play.

After the match, we'd go to a pub, my dad's old Riley car crammed full of freshly scrubbed footballers, and the two of us sitting on their knees. In those days, children were never allowed inside pubs, and so we sat outside on a bench with crisps and lemonade, waiting for our father to emerge and take us home.

I would tease and harass my sister and she would run inside the pub crying, and be driven back out again by the footballers with a promise of more crisps – which I would then eat.

59

My early relationship with my father seems, on reflection, remarkably unremarkable.

But he did already appear to me to be unlike other people's fathers, who were for ever fixing things around the house, or washing the car, or making something. My father did none of that. The women did those kind of things in the household in which he grew up. He did not know what to do with a broken toy, or who to call if the drains were blocked, or how to use a screwdriver or a chisel. My mother did know about all that, and I too soon learned to use a saw and a plane, making coarse woodwork objects which I gave as presents to my father, and which he showed off to his friends as if they were fine works of art.

Three of them still sit in his old study, where I am writing these words: a dowelled bookstand which continues to serve its purpose and is full of the works of his friends Ian McEwan and Simon Gray; a seen-better-days, green-felt-lined stationery tray with lots of compartments containing ancient ring reinforcements that have lost their stickiness, plastic tubes of glue that has dried to rubber, keys whose locks will never be identified and rubber bands so friable that they break at a touch. And my favourite, and my father's, a small smiling dragon, made of wooden offcuts, that falls over with just the suspicion of a breeze.

60

I was a large, strong child, who was, however, frequently ill or injured – breaking my shoulder once and my nose twice – and who had trouble staying upright on any playing field. On one occasion I came downstairs from my bed late in the evening with a sore ankle and a high temperature. I was given some aspirin by my parents. The following day my temperature was so high, 105 degrees Fahrenheit, that doctors were briefly concerned that I might not make it.

Eventually, I was diagnosed with a bone-rotting disease called osteomy-elitis, and spent many months in and out of hospital. For those months, it was as if I had been torn out of my normal world, my conventional school-going family existence.

When school was over for the year, my father and siblings went on holiday to Italy, and I stayed at home with my mother. This, at first, seemed quite desperately unfair; made worse by the fact that I had never been apart from the rest of my family before. Things became even more tragic when a new medical regime emerged: each afternoon a district nurse would come over and give me an injection in my bottom – alternate buttocks on alternate days. I somehow saw this as a humiliation, and no one would tell me if it would ever end.

But then, suddenly, in the midst of my illness, it all changed. Like a mir-acle, the house was full of builder-friends of my parents, most of whom also played football for Battersea. They had been called in, while the rest of the family was away, to fix the roof, repair the banisters, replace the sash cords – and I sat talking with them all day. They seemed to enjoy having me to distract them, usually by showing off my knowledge of the capitals of the world.

They would play music, on the radio or on my parents' gramophone. I remember singing along, and dancing on my right leg (my left leg was still swathed in bandages from the surgery on my rotting ankle) to a song with an overtly medical theme: 'Lily the Pink', performed by a band which might have consisted of builders, The Scaffold. The real builders still remember how I would insist this song was played over and over again.

One of them, Peter Doherty, who later became a footballing teammate and a building-site colleague, endeared himself to me for eternity by bringing me a Danish pastry every morning, before he got down to hard work. In his case, this consisted of telling jokes, flirting, and disappearing behind closed doors with the Iranian au pair, my beloved Mahvash. It all seemed to make homesick Mahvash happy too.

Tony White would also come over, and there seemed to be a continuous party in the house, full of loud baritone laughter, and my contralto mother chirping away happily with all these visitors. Suddenly my absence from the Italian holiday, and the absence of my siblings and my father from the house, became less of a sadness. Indeed, it was more of a golden moment, when I was no longer just one of three – and I had the full attention of everybody.

61

Like my father, I found schoolwork easy. But unlike him, Maths was my forte. Indeed, for a while, I was uncannily good at arithmetic. I was also confident beyond reason, and incorrigible, and bad-tempered. For this, at the age of eight, I was expelled from primary school.

A teacher, Miss Metcalfe, once dared to say I had got a sum wrong, and when she refused to accept that she had, in fact, made a mistake, I became uncontrollably angry. Two male teachers were called and they picked me up; a tall red-haired man called Mr Streak took hold of my legs, and another long-forgotten teacher grabbed my arms. And like that they transported me, at full stretch, through the school, and screaming at the top of my voice ('Stop it, stop it', I can still hear my own cries), to the headmaster's room. There I began to tussle, physically, with the headmaster – who then threatened to beat me. I stopped, and collapsed, in sobs.

My mother was called, and took me away. She bought me an ice cream, and took me shopping, and that evening my father treated me as if I was some kind of wounded but victorious soldier. My mother told me I had to apologise to my teacher; I said I would only do so if she admitted her mistake. So I did say sorry, and she owned up to her error, and all was well until the following year, when another incident occurred, with a different teacher, and I was asked, with little ceremony, to leave.

I think both my parents liked a certain subversive quality that they saw in me, even if they were a little worried. They felt sorry for the beleaguered Miss Metcalfe, who was clearly not very good at Maths. They disliked the pompous headmaster ('Mr Boon, the fat Baboon', according to our pre-juvenile playground chant) almost as much as I did.

My parents were summoned to Mr Boon's office at one point, where he told them that I should be sent to a psychiatrist. 'No child of mine,' my father responded, 'is going to a shrink.' I am fond of these words of my father's: they're full of love and full of protection, and, though I may be reading too much into this, they seem to reflect his complex attitude to conformity and conventionality, as if he felt it would be the psychiatrist's purpose to turn me into a 'normal' child. But, of course, it's also possible that a few visits to a psychiatrist might have done me some good.

62

Decades later, my wife would blame my many shortcomings and stubbornnesses on the way my parents had rewarded and not punished me for my unspeakable behaviour.

63

At the age of nine, I had been cast out of a school which, though no Eden, was walking distance from my home, and which my sister still attended, and which contained, within its red-brick walls, every one of my friends.

I was sent instead to a place where I knew nobody – a fee-paying institution in west London, where we had to wear a uniform and where teachers would hit small children. Not vice versa. I soon found a friend there, though, who was more of a rebel than me. After school, we would ask tube train drivers if we could travel in their cabs, and they always let us, and for a while this seemed like the most exciting thing in the world, as the trains punched their way through the darkness to the bright lights of the next station.

My friend grew bored with trains, and told me about alcohol and girls. He took me through, in word alone, the full gamut of sexual positions; their increasing complexity and uncertain purpose was more than bewildering. And we went out smashing windows in derelict buildings, hanging out with older boys whose greatest pleasure seemed to be drinking their parents' whisky, and then vomiting it out on their parents' carpets. My friend was then expelled from the school, and I was warned by the head teacher of the dangers of 'keeping bad company'. I vowed to myself and to my parents that I would behave. And so, by and large, I did.

I took up rugby, as my father had taken up football, and became a devotee. I played for my school, and my father sometimes came along and stood on the touchlines as I had done for him. I was a below-average player; a clumsy, beefy and sluggish prop forward in a very good rugby team, so good that I would repeatedly report back to my father that we had won by an enormous margin, sixty-nil, or more. And my father could be counted on to say – another one of those phrases or jokes or teases that he would repeat a hundred times and more – 'So were you playing the blind school again?'

The two of us would also now sit and watch rugby for hours together – and I was the expert, and he the tyro, asking what were, in my view, foolish questions about the laws of the game.

64

My father also encouraged me in my schoolboy interest in history, and gave me, as a twelve-year-old, books that were clearly intended for people much older than me, for university students, for people like my father; the type of books which were being reviewed in the magazines he edited.

I may have struggled to understand these books fully, but I liked it that my father thought I might understand them. However much he teased me, I never felt that he (and this is an etymologically awkward word to use here) patronised me. From my childhood, he would talk to me as if he and I were of a similar age – and he let me feel that I might even be as interesting a person to talk to as an adult. For some children this was terrifying. For me, and a few others, it seemed to make everything possible.

He still treated me as a child, pulling my earlobes, and using my nick-names, but he listened closely to what I might say, with what seemed like genuine interest and curiosity. I realise now that many people do not get that feeling from their fathers.

65

In 1967, Karl Miller was put in charge of the *Listener* magazine, owned by the BBC. He'd left the job of literary editor of the *New Statesman* in something of a storm, quarrelling with the overall editor, who complained that one of my father's regular contributors was almost unintelligible. My father resigned. He would face similar struggles at *The Listener*, as he did battle with a conservative readership (Auden accused him of having 'ruined *The Listener*') and the BBC's bureaucracy. It's from this period that I first remember my father as a working man.

Sometimes I went to his wood-panelled office in the Langham, originally and now once again a hotel, where I was given a seat and table at which I drew pictures, and where sweets would be pressed on me by his secretary. And once a week, early in the morning, a large black chauffeur-driven car would arrive outside Limerston Street to take my father to the printers. The chauffeur would let me into the car while my father was getting ready and he showed me how to use its built-in telephone. It seemed very grand, and I boasted at school about my important father who had a telephone in his car. No one – it was the early 1970s – believed that such a thing could exist.

66

When I was about thirteen, to the delight and astonishment of my family
I began to take an interest in cookery. But I would cook nothing simple.
My father had retired as a footballer, and so Sundays were free. I would
look at my mother's cookbooks, or at recipes in colour magazines, and
search for dishes which were very complicated, and had foreign names,
and which took an age to prepare and cook. One of my earliest meals
was chicken *en croute*, in which a whole chicken was encased in pastry.
But my *pièce de résistance* was something known as *pasteles* – tiny pies
filled with pine kernels and minced meat, and they were my father's
favourites – remembered long after I had given up haute cuisine.

I had one notable failure: my attempt to make a bouillabaisse. I
searched several fishmongers for the different kinds of fish and seafood
mentioned in the recipe, and made a stock out of some heads and tails.
But something went wrong with the next stage, with the rouille. The
soup curdled, and it looked terrible – and tasted only slightly better. My
family ate it up, but teased me.

67

We had a visitor for dinner that evening: Tony White, with a plaster cast
that covered the length of his right leg. He'd been injured at football,
playing for Battersea. He, unlike my family, was very gracious about my
failed bouillabaisse.

That was the last time any of us would see Tony. In early January
1976, he died. He had a blood clot, caused by his broken leg, which
killed him. My parents were heartbroken, woebegone. I remember

coming into the sitting room, which we children rarely used. My mother was shaking with tears, and my father was comforting her – and they told me together, their voices overlapping, that Tony had died. I felt like an intruder, and said how sorry I was and retreated from the room.

68

We all went to Tony's funeral – my first – on 20 January 1976. It was a cremation, and I watched, transfixed by the logistics of death, as the coffin slid magically from its resting place through a hatch in the wall; I thought I could see some flames lapping at the coffin.

I was more intrigued than desolate – though desolation could be seen on the faces of almost everyone there. I wanted to know what actually happened to the coffin, and the brass handles, and whether they were burnt too. And I discovered that Tony was really called Anthony John Nigel – and thought he was very wise to shorten his name, as I too had done.

My father could not take the whole day off, and so he left afterwards with my sister and brother who had to go back to school. I stayed with my mother, and we were driven to the wake, held in an old pub called Becky's Dive, beside some railway arches near Waterloo.

I entered a strangely adult world in Becky's Dive – of drunken, grief-stricken grown-ups, who hugged and teased each other, and told stories, while they gradually lost control of their bodies and their words. It was dark and cold inside because Becky had closed her Dive some months earlier, and opened it only for the funeral of a favourite. There was a big hole in the floor, with steps that led down to the beer cellar and the only working toilet. One tipsy friend stumbled and fell – as if she were trying to join Tony White in the underworld. I felt I was invisible there, the only child amidst a sea of grieving adults. Much later, I would discover that I had been noticed.

2014:3

The hospital next to our family house used to be known as St Stephen's – a red-brick Victorian neo-gothic creation, with spires and towers, and long, gloomy wards covered in once-white tiles.

In my childhood, it was famous as the hospital where a patient woke up from an operation and pointed out, quite correctly, that the wrong leg had been amputated. St Stephen's was pulled down in the 1990s, and replaced by the glass-and-steel Chelsea and Westminster Hospital. A place of modernity, we thought, in its airy design and with its displays – mural and pendulous – of contemporary art and, we hoped, a pioneer in modern medicine. And for passers-by there is even street theatre of a sort: for outside the main entrance, in all weathers, is a living tableau of smoker-patients, clad in nightgowns and slippers, drawing on cigarettes as if they were their last and blocking the pavement with their drip stands and their wheelchairs. Some will wave or chat; others seem buried in a fog of sickness.

We, as a family, know the hospital all too well. Two of my mother's knees and one of mine were rebuilt here. And my father was the most regular of visitors – to our hospital bedsides but mostly as an inmate and outpatient. On one occasion, in the Chelsea and Westminster for a minor operation, he was assigned to a ward with a window from which he could look down into his own bedroom.

We spoke of stringing up a line with a pulley from the house up to the ward, so we could deliver basketfuls of goodies to his bedside without having to make the five-minute walk round the corner to the entrance of the hospital

The hospital became almost a second home – or an extension of the existing one, separated from us only by a garden wall. As a teenager, my brother had climbed that wall and returned with the top half of a human being, in the form of an anatomical model. All its parts – brain, lungs, hearts, kidneys, intestines – were fully detachable, and as we children soon found out, very hard to put back. My father adopted the model, as if it were a child who would never leave home. It stayed with him to the last in his bedroom – to the consternation of some visitors, who saw its presence as a mark of extreme eccentricity.

In his memoirs, my father described his room as having a 'definite morbidity'. The 'poor man', as we all called the model, was the star exhibit, but there was also the portrait in oil of a young man we all knew well who had killed himself, and an old print of women and children working down a mine in Gilmerton, where he grew up. 'I like to lie,' he wrote, 'as if in my coffin, amidst such memorabilia.'

After the 'King Lear evening', the oncologists and the radiologists gave up attempting to cure my father, and so the experts in dying took over. And on the afternoon of 8 April 2014, the pattern of a lifetime was reversed when a doctor from the hospital, a consultant in palliative care, made the five-minute walk from the hospital to our home. I let her in. She was a breezy, straightforward woman who stopped to admire the paintings and the books that conceal the inner walls of our home.

My father had known she was coming and had planned to ask her questions, such as 'How ill am I?', which he had written down on a piece of paper, and which he lost several times in the hours before she turned up. My mother and I had decided that we would leave him alone with the doctor for this difficult part of the conversation. But he was not at his best when she came and his questions went unasked, by him at least. He was asleep almost the whole time she was there.

After examining my father, the doctor came downstairs and sat at our kitchen table with my mother and me, and had a cup of tea and a biscuit. She was friendly, talking about herself and her family, and asked us how we were managing with my father. My mother explained that I had come back from India to help look after him, and that my older brother was also staying in the house, and that my sister came over almost every day. All the children were around, and lots of grandchildren. My mother used the word 'lucky' to describe herself and my father.

The conversation did soon turn to my father's health. She smiled as she told us first how my father had only woken briefly during her examination to complain of a pain in 'the fetlock'. She was amused by the use of this word, no longer part of general medical parlance, and she struggled to work out which part of his leg he meant. We talked about his pains, and his cancers – and what nursing help we might expect.

She then looked more seriously at the two of us, anxiously looking back at her. 'He's very ill; he's dying,' she said in a still, small voice. We nodded back, knowingly, but not really wanting to know. And I said something foolish about how we were all dying; we just didn't know how long it would take.

She asked us if we wanted to know how long she thought he had to live. We looked at each other, and nodded: hesitant, slow-motion nods. Yes, we did. 'Weeks,' she said, 'a matter of weeks.' I let out an involuntary cry.

PART TWO

69

In 1977, I learned a secret.

The secret was about me, though in another way it didn't really feel that it was about me at all. It was about my parents, and about the man I had always thought of as my father's best friend, Tony White. I learned the secret at the start of the summer holiday. I was fifteen.

My mother and I were painting my bedroom a forbiddingly dark shade of blue, almost indigo, that I had chosen, presumably, to represent my outlook on life. The bed and the floor were covered with old white bed sheets, to protect the carpet and my furniture. I remember feeling a little sick from the smell of paint. My mother told me to drink some milk to line my stomach. I left the room, and walked along the corridor to the kitchen and pulled an unopened bottle of milk from the fridge. I removed the silver cap by pressing it down with my thumb, and drank, as I always did, straight from the bottle – swallowing the full pint.

I returned to the bedroom and leaned over to pick up the paintbrush again. My mother said, with a slight catch in her voice, 'There's something I want to tell you.' I turned to her, a dripping paintbrush in my hand.

'Your real father is… was Tony White.'

I remember responding with silence, which seemed to linger as my mother waited for some kind of reaction from me. The blue paint dripped onto the white sheet, and I stared, hypnotised by the spiral pattern it made.

70

Once spoken, of course, my mother's words could not be retracted. And those words set off a slow-motion cascade of feelings and reactions and consequences. More of that to follow.

71

First, the story – in its striking brevity. My mother, at the time, told me the thinnest of tales – that she'd had a 'love affair' with Tony, and that I was the result. She said that my father knew about this from before I was born, and had always loved me as his own.

72

It took many more years before I began to piece together a more complete story, about my paternity and about the complex triangular relationship between my parents, Jane and Karl Miller, and Tony White, my biological father.

This is not because my mother deliberately held back any information. In fact, in those early years after I was told the secret, my mother was keener than I to talk about Tony and her and Karl. Much later, I would be more inquisitive. She was and still can be reticent about talking about the more intimate side of her involvement with these two men – but then few parents want to talk about their sex lives with their children, and even fewer children want to hear. She has, tremulously at times, given her backing to this project, an attempt by me to narrate and make sense of this story, and to understand in particular my father's axial role in the events it describes.

73

A great deal went unsaid, for many decades.

For example, it wasn't until late in the life of my father that he and I felt able to discuss my paternity. And it was only after his death, while going through his carefully organised papers, that I came across letters from Tony White which gave me a clearer picture of how the three of them navigated the uncertainties and tensions of this relationship, and were able to remain close to each other.

I felt my father's death freed me to talk more openly about the secret. This is partly because, in my father's own words to me, he had for decades, felt 'too shy' to talk about it. And he worried that any attempt to discuss the issue might 'wound'. He meant wound me, but it might have wounded him, too. I no longer think public knowledge of this story wounds either of us, or my mother. And for those who remember Tony White, and there are many who still do, this story may provide some solace.

This then is my version not only of the story of Karl and Jane, but also of Tony, and of how I came to be. And to tell that story, I will need to rewind a little.

Unlike my father, Tony White left no memoirs. But many of his letters, and a few, sporadic diary entries, have survived. So have hundreds of photographs, several biographical fragments (including one by my father), as well as the often adoring, mythologising memories of his many friends. I have not always, as someone entangled in this story by blood and sentiment, found it easy to separate truth from legend in the life of Tony White.

His early death, and his many circles of friends, and his medium-sized troop of secret and half-secret lovers, have colluded consciously and subconsciously to create the image of a man who was more than human; Christ-like, if you listen to some of his closest admirers.

One of those admirers repeats a story, perhaps a Chinese whisper, supposedly overheard at a London literary party.

> It seems that every generation has its own version of the Christ figure, and so, apparently, has ours. People who were at Cambridge in the early 1950s talk about him a good deal. They say he was a brilliant actor being groomed for stardom at the Old Vic, when he gave up acting to take a job as a gas-lamp lighter in the slums. It was the daring thing for

a well-educated young man of the time to do – chuck up everything and just clear off. He died rather young, killed in a game of soccer. I believe he was called Tony White.

This kind of talk, with its kernel of truth, and its flesh of hagiography, makes writing about Tony a less than straightforward task. He was not a saint, nor a Messiah, but he did choose an unconventional path, and in his grown-up years he did much to cover his tracks. He is also hero-worshipped by most of the dying breed who knew him well; the authors of what might be called the Ballad of Tony White.

76

Tony was born in 1930, a year before my father, and two years before my mother. Unlike my father, but like my mother, he was brought up in a middle-class nuclear family – one of three children who lived with their parents. For much of Tony's childhood they lived in a big house on Ladbroke Grove in west London.

They were a well-travelled, multilingual family. Tony's older sister, Lois, whom I came to know in recent years, remembers her parents speaking Malay. They'd picked it up while they lived in Singapore after the First World War – and used it as a secret language when they didn't want their children to understand what they were saying. Tony's father, known as Heth, was English, spoke French and German (and Malay), and worked first as a trader in the Far East, then in the lace business in Europe and finally as a British civil servant, censoring the press in Germany after the war.

Tony's mother, Yvonne, was French. Lois told me that Heth's family had opposed him marrying a foreigner and then added, as if these facts were directly related (and perhaps they were), that her mother was an unhappy soul, often depressed.

I met Yvonne, crippled by a stroke, just once, in the gloomiest of London nursing homes, not long after my mother told me about Tony. I remember thinking that she was the smallest grown-up I had ever seen. She was very ill by then, and she spoke slowly with a strong French accent. She had not been told about my connection with Tony – but did pay me some attention, and I remember her giving me one hard long enquiring look. She also gave me a Fox's Glacier Mint, which sentimental Sam stashed away as a keepsake. I can't find it now. She died soon after I met her.

Lois said that her mother never recovered from the death of her oldest child, Alan, a poet and an artist, who was killed in 1944 on the last day of the Battle of Monte Cassino.

When Yvonne heard that Tony had died, she told a friend of his that she had 'no more tears left to shed'.

As I begin to write about Tony White, I have become conscious of what might be called an 'equality issue'. Do I, for instance, need to write about Tony's parents in the same way that I have talked about Karl Miller's? More generally, do I need to treat these two fathers of mine with some level of equality?

My easy, instinctive answer is a simple 'No'. I am less interested in Tony himself – and more interested in what he meant to my parents, and (this is secondary) whether he might tell me anything about myself. I have never felt for Tony what I feel for my father.

And yet as I dig around, unearthing ancient Tony-fables, I find there is far more for me to say about Tony than I had anticipated. He has, in a way, filled out. I can imagine him in a way that I could not before, and he has even begun to appear in my dreams.

But the answer is still 'No', and anyway the notion of equality in these circumstances is absurd. Indeed, the question now seems like a foolish one – and really I should erase those last three paragraphs.

79

But I still do want to know more about Tony than I ever did before, and there is something about him and his story that has seduced me.

And I can't help but make occasional comparisons between the two men, my two fathers.

80

Just as Karl Miller was an orphan, so Tony White was half-French. These were the most important facts of their childhood; circumstances that were beyond their control, but that described something fundamental about how they would always see themselves.

The earliest surviving letter I have found from Tony is an unusual document. Written during the Second World War, it is both a period piece, and one of those timeless testimonies to the near-universal frightfulness of being a thirteen-year-old boy who is almost a man. It is additionally a footnote in the history of British public school racism, and in its use of two words – 'jolly' and 'quisling' – is of deeper interest as a case study in historical linguistics. I also like to think the letter gives a sense of the person that Tony would come to be: determined and contrary.

'My darling Mummy,' he begins, and then goes on to describe an argument with a fellow pupil at his new boarding school, Haileybury.

> [He] called me a 'filthy French rat', knowing that I had a French mother, so I jolly well told him I wouldn't stand for that and that he jolly well had better not say that again, and he replied with a good many insults about France and you, and so I jolly well saw red and let fly, and gave him a jolly good bashing up.

Other boys then joined in and attacked Tony.

> They gave me a fearful time of it and nearly knocked the breath out of me and hurt me quite a lot, shouting jeering remarks the whole time. Since then they have been absolutely

beastly, and keep insulting everything to do with France and so on, but I'm jolly well going to stick up like hell for you, Moz darling, whatever they may do or say about you. I shall never let down France or anything French as long as I live. They are our allies, half my family is French, and I hate anyone who calls you and French people 'quislings'…

Well, I must stop now if I want to catch the post.
So cheerio, your devoted Tony

82

I'm intrigued by that quisling reference. It must be one of the first.

In 1943, Norway was under German occupation with a puppet government led by Vidkun Quisling, whose surname had begun to enter the common tongue of many nations, and was already in use by a thirteen-year-old Anglo-French schoolboy. France was, at the time, also under German occupation, with its own puppet French government, and its own quisling.

83

Tony White was skinny and gangling in his early teens. Photos of the time seem to depict him as a gentle soul with the warmest of smiles, and it's hard to imagine him giving anyone a 'jolly good bashing up'.

He soon filled out. Adolescence, cross-country runs and chest-expanders conspired to turn him into a bear-like human, with the same smile, but with the calves and thighs and shoulders of a small giant. I would inherit those features.

84

Lois described her brother as a normal, conventional child obsessed with cricket – who became, from her point of view, distinctly unconventional as he became an adult. 'A hippy before they existed,' she later told me, a judgement that would be echoed by others, and not always appreciatively. She thought that living in Germany in the late 1940s – doing his National Service, teaching soldiers to drive trucks – had a profound impact on Tony. She couldn't quite say why, but she used the word 'democratic', as if his army years had taught him to be friends with people from different social backgrounds.

Lois described herself as the opposite of Tony, and I wonder if this resulted from different responses to their mixed heritage. She refused to speak French as a teenager, and she told me she hated the fact that her mother was a foreigner. She wanted to be 'normal'; she didn't want to 'stand out'. Tony was bilingual and took great pleasure in his French connection. He never minded being different.

85

Tony would later be legendary among his friends for his reticence and discretion about his complicated love life. They knew not to ask.

But as a teenager he wrote long screeds to his closest friend, John Holmstrom, about his crushes – his romantic attachments to his fellow schoolboys. In this period, and into his early twenties, Tony had a series of relationships with young men, which were undoubtedly sexual in intent, if not always in practice.

By the time he got to Cambridge, he seems to have taken the decision, announced in a letter to the same friend, that he would henceforward be heterosexual, or at least much more heterosexual than he had been before. However, many of his closest male friends were gay, or bisexual – and it's clear that he continued to have intense and intimate relationships with both men and women – even if he actually had sex with men very rarely.

He once told my mother, to her discomfort, that men moved him more than women.

At school, Tony wrote poetry, and began to act – declaring it his life's wish both to write and to be on the stage.

None of his poems survive, but John Holmstrom remembered Tony as 'a firm believer of the link between love and poetry'. Holmstrom, a fine poet himself and much admired by my father, described Tony's poems as:

> conventionally poetic skeletons decked out with grim Websterian jewels, but they were far from the usual 'I laid my chest / upon your breast' stuff. It was easy to point out clichés and suggest improvement – and he accepted most of them with great good humour.

At Cambridge, Tony put aside his poems, and emerged as an actor of promise, a tough romantic hero whose performances in classic roles such as Cyrano de Bergerac, Romeo and Berowne would be remembered by his peers many decades later.

My father, in one of several lyrical descriptions of Tony in his memoirs, described him as 'one of the dangerous new belt-buckle youth, and a very good romantic actor, who gave all his sweet nature to Cyrano and Berowne.'

Thom Gunn said that Tony played each of his roles as if they all had the 'romantic-existentialist' character that defined Tony himself. He was unusual, Thom argued, in portraying Romeo as 'a tough'.

It's clear from these two accounts of Tony's acting, written by his closest friends of the time, that he had a tendency to play himself on stage.

88

Thom and Tony, spurred on by my father, borrowed the word 'panache' from *Cyrano de Bergerac*, and converted it into a key part of what Thom would later refer to as their 'home-spun philosophy'; 'a mélange,' he explained, 'of Rostand, Stendhal, Shakespeare and Camus.'

Tony became the 'Prince of Panache'. For my father, writing almost forty years later, '"Panache" was a word and a mode of the time and the place, and its prince was Tony White, saluted as a local avatar, a fine ideal of tender toughness.' Thom, meanwhile, described Tony as 'a man of courtesy', and added that he meant 'courtesy not merely in a social sense, it was a giving of himself, in all his strength and sweetness, to others'.

I'm interested by the language used in these descriptions of Tony, written after his death, by Karl Miller and Thom Gunn. It is almost Arthurian. And perhaps Tony is Sir Lancelot.

And one more thing, though my father would hate me saying this, it does all seem rather homoerotic.

89

My father first set eyes on Tony White while the latter was on stage, playing the butch gay lover of an English king. He was Gaveston, both the hero and villain of Marlowe's *Edward II*, and photographs of that performance show him foppishly dressed, with jewelled gloves, the tightest of trousers, and a confident sneer on his upper lip.

My father stuck the playbill for *Edward II* into his scrapbook alongside a review which described Tony's performance as one of 'most admirably managed rhetoric'. By the end of the academic year they were fast friends, both studying English under F.R. Leavis at the same college. But Tony had little time for revising between rehearsals and so switched for his final year to French, a subject where he would have, linguistically speaking, a head start over his fellow students. That was his final year; the year of Romeo, Cyrano and panache. It was also the only year when Tony and both my parents were at Cambridge together.

90

My mother met both Tony and Karl, the fathers of her children, at different Cambridge parties hosted by the same person. Tony first, in January 1952, when she was still a schoolgirl, visiting her friend Sasha. She remembers him as 'beautiful and attentive and kind', someone who took pity on a youngster in a crowd of Cambridge students who all seemed to know each other. They talked in an easy, relaxed way – and the following year, with my mother now a student, they became part of each other's outer circles.

My mother, too, liked to act – and performed alongside Tony in the French play *Britannicus*. They were each other's love interest, but it was the most chaste of dramas: no clinches and no kisses. This lack of intimacy was matched off-stage, for several years, at least.

My mother met my father some nine months after she met Tony, also at a Sasha party, to celebrate her arrival in Cambridge. A year and a bit later they were a couple, and in 1956, they got married.

91

Tony and my father remained close friends in this period, the mid-fifties, and wrote to each other regularly. Several of Tony's letters and postcards survive, carefully filed away by my father in some old wooden drawers kept close to his desk. The letters are filed by date, not author. But Tony's idiosyncratic handwriting ensures that his stand out. He almost always writes in black – with tall, upright pen strokes, ubiquitous colons, and lower case '*e*'s shaped like little capitals – '*E*'s not '*e*'s – as if he'd missed a primary school lesson in joined-up writing.

The earliest letters touch gently on their love lives: Tony tells my father to remember him to an old flame in Cambridge, and asks with concern about his relationship with Sasha.

There's a playful tone to these letters. In the first, written while they were both on their Easter holidays from Cambridge – my father with his aunts in Scotland, and Tony with his parents in Germany – Tony imagines Karl Miller as an 'old hermit' in his 'hoose' in Edinburgh, while he is eating 'fat juicy steaks and drinking wine quotidinially' in Koblenz.

92

The second letter, written in October 1953, after Tony had left Cambridge but while my father was still there, is more confessional and nostalgic in tone.

Tony has just had a setback. At the time, he seemed to be on the verge of becoming a film star, spoken of as the next Richard Burton. His friends believed he was a shoo-in as Romeo for what would become the Rank

Organisation's 1954 film version of the play. The screen test had gone well: he was on a shortlist of two actors. But he wasn't chosen.

He didn't hide his disappointment from my father, but then bouncily declared that he was off to look for work to clear his 'large overdraft'; 'you see I'm more practical than you.' And he then becomes oblique, switching into character, Richard II in this case and not Romeo: 'My rash fierce blaze of riot (if it invites such a title) is over and I'm for the gray days. Now quit self-pity'. That final sentence is directed at himself.

Tony is already missing Cambridge, and his friends. In the same letter, he is full of playful, teasing excitement for my father at the start of his new academic year. 'You'll be venerated, flattered, worshipped ad nauseam... The horizon is blue, Karl, it's very blue indeed – & I shall come down one day and rake you over, swollen and languorous as you will be, G.O.M of the Cambridge literary world, sole imperator and Great General.'

Amidst the joshing humour, there was melancholy too; and at the very end of his letter he reveals how he feels about his failure to become a film star, and his departure from Cambridge, with the words, 'It's all so sad, Karl.'

93

Like my father, Tony loved his time at Cambridge. He was a star there, and would never be such a star again.

Soon after he failed to get the role of Romeo (he referred to the decision as 'rank cowardice' or a 'lack of rank foolhardiness' in a letter to

John Holmstrom), he considered giving up acting entirely. But he got a job at the Old Vic theatre company and had two good years playing lesser roles in classic plays with well-known actors: Cassio to Richard Burton's Othello, for instance.

94

Tony took the theatre very seriously, more so than most of his contemporaries, but came to despise most actors. He believed in the transformative power of great drama, and his own potential to convey important ideals through his acting. However, he wasn't sure that he wanted to lead an actor's life.

At Cambridge, he'd been able to pick and choose his parts, and as he put it, 'impose terms'. At the Old Vic, he was just one of many. Among his letters to John Holmstrom, there is this wonderfully theatrical rant on the subject.

> It's terribly silly, really, I suppose, but having got exactly what I wanted, the Old Vic, I'm starting to have terrible qualms and think I must be barmy to go on the stage...
>
> Actors are, with so few exceptions, so vain and squishy – the prospect is terrifying. Won't I be warped and sickened by theatrical chit-chat, hard luck stories, petty vanities and jealousies, nervous disorders and heavens know what else?

And how can I be sure that my ideals are necessarily those that I am capable of embodying in the theatre – might I not convey just those things that I loathe in other actors? There's something so fucking cushy and effete about it, which makes me quayle and quake – human beings in cellophane, in showcases, afraid of being tired, cut, dirty, smelly, disfigured, in a word, real – because they must be bloody lovely puppets every night.

Tony lasted two seasons at the Old Vic and then in late 1956 he abruptly gave up the theatre. I've been unable to find anything more about that decision, from the records of the Old Vic, from Tony's letters, or from the memories of his friends. But he did have a new job.

95

Tony became, to the consternation and amusement of his friends, a lamplighter in the East End of London.

The March 1957 edition of *Picture Post* magazine carried a double-page spread with photographs, entitled 'Footlights to street lamps', describing how a successful, up-and-coming actor had given up his career and was now a gas lamplighter in and around Billingsgate Market.

One photo shows Tony at daybreak, a big smile in his face, as he rides his bicycle over the cobblestones of an East End street. Leaning on his shoulder is an eight-foot steel torch, like a giant oven-lighter, for igniting the gas lamps. Recently, I looked closely at the photograph for the first time.

He's wearing a brown leather jerkin which I immediately recognised.

I used to wear an identical jerkin in the late seventies. I asked my mother about it. 'Yes, it's the same one.' But she can't remember whether Tony gave it to her, or perhaps she took it from his flat after he died; and she can't remember whether she kept it for me, and whether she encouraged me to wear it, knowing it was his.

It's an unimportant thing, an old leather jerkin, I suppose. But it is important to me. Like the Fox's Glacier Mint, it has long disappeared.

Tony's short-lived employment as one of London's last lamplighters came in for much mockery from his Cambridge friends. Only Tony, they said, would take up a job with such obviously limited career prospects, since, they pointed out, electric street lights had replaced gas almost everywhere. But he was, at the same time, admired by some as a Romantic hero in the making, who was doing what no one else dared. The lamplighter episode became an early verse in the 'Ballad of Tony White'.

In fact, a careful reading of the text of the *Picture Post* article provides a more logical explanation for Tony's decision to become a lamplighter. Lamplighters only need to work for a brief period each day, at sunrise and sunset, and that leaves plenty of time for Tony to write – which, he says, is his real reason for giving up acting. I approve of this logic, and I would quite like to become a lamplighter myself.

My father was in America for the entire period that Tony spent at the Old Vic, and in the two letters that have survived Tony talks little about acting, or lamplighting, or writing. What is notable about the letters for me, as I examine them microscopically, is the attention he pays to my mother.

In the first letter, my parents are not yet married and my mother is about to leave for Boston to join my father. Tony tells my father that Jane was looking 'very ravishing' when he last saw her at a London party, and he declares that we all felt 'great joy' to hear that she was going to America, as 'we are all sure you're not eating properly and American girls are notoriously cold'. He then suggests that my mother may not have been particularly friendly towards him when they last met.

> You are going to have your hands full as Jane is going to be bitterly intolerant about the Yanks, I can't help feeling, or is she only severe on her fellow countrymen?

My mother cannot remember anything that might have caused this complaint.

98

Tony's second letter is still more striking. It purports to be a simple message of congratulations on hearing of my parents' marriage – but it is open, particularly in retrospect, to alternative readings.

'Dear Karl,' he begins, uncontroversially, writing more than five weeks after the wedding,

> I should have answered your letter way back and I should have written to you as soon as I heard you were married – neither of which I have done. Forgive me.
>
> What can I say? Except that I was absolutely delighted to hear the news and if you and Jane aren't utterly happy, there will be no illusions left to me – you are hand-picked. I have drunk your health quietly in bachelor pubs, and suddenly felt myself to be a tired, old, balding slightly grotesque alley-cat.

But if I don't wish you well, not well but the best of best, I don't wish anyone well.

Following that array of hand-picked double negatives, Tony then gives my father his more general opinion of marriage, with a parenthetical remark which had me clucking with disbelief the first time I read it.

Most marriages seem to be such a terrible waste of one or other person (usually because one wants the person oneself, perhaps).

He continues with another compliment for my mother

With great unselfishness (for Jane was looking as radiant a woman as ever when I saw her just before leaving)... I can say in all sureness, this marriage is the rare exception and gives me such pleasure to think on.

And Tony rounds off this part of the letter by suggesting, in a round-about but remarkably prescient way, that what was so good about this particular marriage is that it didn't exclude him. My parents were not just old acquaintances from Cambridge, but individuals who both belonged to his inner circle of friendship.

I'd have been so uneasy to imagine either of you married to some lousy twat and not because you are both of 'the circle' but because you are of my *personal* circle.

I try hard not to read too much into this letter, but it does seem to indicate that, subconsciously at least, Tony was wondering just where he fitted into this marital relationship.

When my parents returned to London from America, they saw a lot of Tony. My mother's diaries reveal that he often used to drop by after dinner, especially when the birth of my older brother in July 1957 made it harder for my parents to go out in the evenings. The main subject of conversation, according to my mother, was football.

In late 1956, Tony and my father had, along with a boyfriend of Sasha's, founded Battersea Park football team. Just five people turned up for the first match, so Sasha was co-opted in goal for one of the teams in a three-a-side match. Not long after, my mother, pregnant with my older brother, made her one and only appearance for Battersea, as a rather immobile and hesitant goalkeeper. Soon they were able to pull together a full team, and began playing competitively.

Tony White kept a scrapbook about the team he co-founded with my father, full of match reports, season updates, team sheets, press cuttings and photos. It was given to my father after Tony died.

Inside the front cover, Tony has stuck the only photograph of the three of them – Jane and Karl and Tony – that I have been able to find. It's a slightly unexpected picture to find here, because they're not play-ing football, and are not wearing football kit – though in the background there are friends of theirs who are properly kitted out.

It was taken in Hyde Park, with the three of them seated on the grass: Tony leans back and looks confidently straight at the camera; my father leans forward and is turning towards the photographer as if his name has just been called, while my mother is slightly out of focus, almost lying down, reclining on her elbows. She thinks she may have been looking at her new baby. Why and when did Tony choose this photo for the inside cover of his football scrapbook?

I've found two more letters from Tony to my father, from the period before the three of them have a holiday together in Rome in 1958. My mother told me that I am being too forensic and deterministic in my reading of these letters. I replied that it's a good sign that we don't agree on everything.

One of the letters is undated, but the context suggests that it was written in 1957. My father is a civil servant at the Treasury at the time, and despondent, and Tony is encouraging him to do something more suited to his talents. It's a letter full of flattery, and encouragement – tinted, as always, with a little teasing,

> You happen to be, worse luck, one of the two, three, and at a squeeze four people on this earth for whose souls I can register more than indifference... Therefore one of the few feelings I still have is resentment that your soul does not clap its hands and sing and louder sing, when so many shrivelled dates of souls are giving forth shrill whines and being toasted (toasted dates – delicious!)... If I had a modest slice of your talent I'd cry 'Hallelujah': as it is I've barely enough for the tiniest 'Hail Mary'.

It ends with a warm mention for my mother: 'Love to that most enduring [sic] and wonderful wife of yours'. And he signs off with a Scottish tease, 'Yours aye, McWhite.'

The second letter, dated 4 August 1958, was sent from the small island of Inishbofin off the coast of Connemara in the west of Ireland. Tony had been on Inishbofin for three weeks, and would spend large parts of the rest of his life staying there, or on the mainland opposite the island.

Tony had gone to Ireland to write, and had rented an entirely empty cottage. He described how he had created chairs from boulders, and fires for cooking from driftwood. 'It is good,' he wrote, 'to get to know the Robinson Crusoe in oneself – how to light a fire with a safety pin and a bootlace.'

But the letter is really about their forthcoming holiday in Italy. Tony is planning to take a boat from Ireland to France and then travel overland to Rome, where he hoped to meet my parents. He asks for a quick postcard from my father, to say exactly where they would be staying.

He signed off by returning, tangentially, to the theme of his earlier congratulatory letter by describing, separately, both my mother and father as 'much-envied'.

102

Tony arrived in Rome on 7 September and spent much of the next twelve days with my parents. They had already been there for ten days, having deposited my one-year-old brother with my father's aunts in Edinburgh. They all stayed in a large flat on Via Giulia, while its normal occupants were staying in my parents' much smaller flat in London.

My mother remembers being teased a lot by my father and Tony – about her love of sightseeing (the two men boasted that they had set a record for seeing the Sistine Chapel in the shortest possible time), and about how often her bottom was pinched by Italian men. They ate and drank well, and together they visited, according to my mother's diary, the Vatican Museum, the coastal resort of Ostia and the Rome zoo.

They also all went to a football match at the Olympic Stadium and saw one of my father's favourite players, the Welshman John Charles, turning out for Juventus against the local team Lazio. John Charles was known by Juventus fans as 'Testa d'Oro', 'head of gold', and this, somehow, became my father's new nickname for Tony. Then on Friday 19 September 1958 my father left; his holidays were over, and he had to return to work in London.

Tony and my mother were on their own in Rome.

2014:4

We did not tell my father what the doctor had told us: that he would probably be dead within weeks. I suppose we just couldn't bear the idea of doing so; and on that day, and the ones that followed, he showed little sign of being able to make any sense of such information.

But I could not stop turning the doctor's words over and over in my mind. At the time I had pressed her further. 'What will he die of, then, *in a matter of weeks?*' I asked, repeating her words back to her. 'I don't know', she said, 'there are still many things we don't understand about death, and how it actually happens.' She described the way in which organs almost seem to conspire with each other to stop working. 'That will probably be what happens to Karl – his body will slowly shut down.' I liked her honesty, and the way she said Karl as if she had known him for years, but I couldn't quite believe that he was so close to death.

After she left, I regretted that I had not asked her precisely what she meant by 'weeks'. I went into autistic overdrive in my attempts to interpret what I began to call her 'death sentence', though it was less a sentence, and more of a sub-clause. 'Weeks', I argued to myself, clearly meant less than 'months', so presumably she meant less than two months. It followed, therefore, that the good doctor was predicting that my father would be dead within seven weeks. I went to my week-at-a-view diary, and turned over seven pages. And at the top of the seventh page, I wrote 'Dd?' This stood, I'm afraid, for 'Dad dead?'

The first ten days after the doctor's visit were pretty desperate. I now realise that we would each grasp at the slightest sign that my father was getting better, that the doctor might be wrong. It was sometimes a half-conversation, or an endearment from my father's lips, or that he expressed a desire to shave, or for a chocolate biscuit. But each time we thought we had spotted an improvement, he deteriorated again just as quickly.

But then, something happened – and my father did begin to emerge from his miasma. He began to sleep less and talk more. Sometimes, I would read to him from his own writings, as if to prod and tease him into full consciousness. In his study, which I was now using, I had found old copies of Schola Regia, his school magazine. It was the only one of his many magazines in which he had published his own poetry. He was embarrassed by his juvenilia, and kept trying to silence me – particularly when others came into the room – but then suddenly he would join in, remembering the next line as I read it out.

There was one poem entitled 'Elegy' that I liked above all others – partly, I think, because it seemed to deal with his current situation, and with the prospect of death. The poem begins with questions that my teenage father might be asking of himself as an old man.

> Why do your eyes darken with the slow shades
> Of the lengthening night: why do your tears
> Fall with the fall to earth of autumn leaves
> Drifting like dust in the memory of the years?

The questioning resumes towards the end of the poem, with words that seemed to catch something of my father's parlous condition, autumnal and haunted:

> Why sorrow for the holiness of earth,
> When the grey autumn of your life will come,
> And haunt with strangled cry the marshes of
> Your soul, and fail with the setting of the sun.

And the poem concludes with words of wonderfully sagacious gloom, which hold out no prospect of resurrection, just the vacuum of everlasting nothingness.

> Here is no regeneration:
> With the setting of this sun, we find
> The night that is endless.
> Glimpsing the light upon the hills, sensing
> The octopus arms of the flesh, and then
> With one mad blaze of life, you sink deep down
> Into the hungry shadows of your end.
> Age and ageing, the coldness of the grave
> Alone we know; your body shall no more
> Gleam in its whiteness through my mind, but chill
> In the wind of time, and wither to the core.

I wanted my father, terribly, to show me that 'one mad blaze of life': to wake up, to tease me, to belittle my opinions about football, to walk with me round the corner to our favourite delicatessen, to tell me off for being winsome in my writing. And, as it turned out, he would do all these things in the coming months. But at a cost.

One morning, in late April, just after I had finished reading out loud his elegy to death, my father turned to me, and looked me in the eye. 'Poor Sam,' he said, 'you didn't know you were coming back to all this.' I told him with saccharine honesty how glad I was that I had come back, and that I wanted to spend as much time as I could with him.

I was not at all prepared for what he said next.

'Would you,' he asked, 'think less of me if I killed myself?' I did not respond immediately. I did not discuss (and I regret this) what I think he wanted to discuss, in his circumlocutory way: namely, that he wanted to die, and that he wasn't sure how to go about killing himself.

Instead, I gurgled some blandishment about not being foolish, and changed the subject. But I had begun to realise the different kind of pain caused to my father by his improving health. He now knew how ill he was, and that, at least some of the time, he wished he was dead.

103

For decades, I believed that the relationship between my mother and Tony White began and ended, more or less, with my conception in the spring of 1961. This wasn't the case. And only recently did my mother begin to tell me, rather shyly, about their Roman holiday.

They first kissed on the balcony of the flat on Via Giulia in Rome, not long after my father left for London. She describes herself now as having been 'terribly innocent' – in the sense of naive – but insists there was no seduction, or premeditation, or unwillingness on the part of either of them. 'It just happened,' she told me in a voice that seemed to shut down this line of questioning. They had two days alone together. It rained a lot, she said. And she recalled Tony comforting her as she wept: she was missing her one-year-old son, and felt guilty about having left him behind.

104

Then her friend Sasha turned up, as planned – and once again there were three of them. They kept their relationship secret from Sasha, but she seems to have guessed. On her deathbed, forty years later, long after Tony had died, Sasha asked my mother about her friendship with Tony – and she told her about me.

The three of them: Sasha, Tony and my mother then went to Sicily where Sasha was making a BBC documentary. My mother found a photo recently, the only one that shows her and Tony alone together, taken in Sicily, presumably by Sasha. They're sitting next to each other beneath the decorated medieval cloisters of the cathedral of Monreale. Tony is in a white T-shirt staring at the camera with a sleepy confidence and a satisfied smile. My mother's hair has been pulled back under a headscarf, and she wears a long-sleeved striped shirt and a white skirt that has ridden above her knees. She's also looking straight ahead, a half smile on her lips, but the rest of her face is unreadable – because the photo has been folded so that her eyes are now obscured, permanently, by wrinkles of bromide. They could almost be a couple on honeymoon.

My mother and Tony travelled back together from Sicily to London by train (and boat), and my mother kept the tickets, both in the name of White, and stashed them away in secret along with photographs and postcards from the holiday.

They agreed that she should tell my father about their affair. She's not sure why they wanted to tell him, but that it just felt like the right thing to do. My mother says my father reacted with little obvious emotion, or even surprise, and made it clear that he did not want to discuss the matter. She then went straight to Scotland to collect my brother.

Tony, meanwhile, returned to the west coast of Ireland and to a job supervising a lobster farm, having sent a short, sad note to my father with a cheque repaying a small loan.

> Dear Karlo,
> Here is what I reckon up as owing you, from borrowings.
> I wish I could see you before I go: but time is short, and any-
> way my heart is so full of conflict, I'd be rendered silent.
> The only emotion, constant and identifiable, is one of
> gratefulness to you. About the rest – I'm sure Jane will have
> told you by now – the less said by me the better.
> I'll write you from exile...

This was just the first in a series of what are, to me, extraordinary letters written by Tony White. Each of them was part of an attempt to repair, even strengthen, a friendship. But there was no question of Tony grovelling to my father, or even of apologising for an affair – a fling, really, at this stage – that threatened to break that friendship, and possibly break a marriage.

Indeed, he would soon tell my father, 'I am not sorry for what I have done.' But he still wished, more than anything, that Karl Miller and Tony White could remain friends. No one could accuse Tony of being servile or devious.

107

Two weeks after his return to Ireland, Tony wrote to my father again – at length, this time. Of all his letters to my father, this one tells me most about their friendship.

I must admit that I was taken aback by its contents when I first found the letter, after my father died – stunned, I think, by its bluntness. I have now read it many times over, painstakingly pondering its meaning almost as if it were an ancient text deserving of critical exegesis and learned commentary. And, in retrospect, I realise that it was the discovery of this letter, and the ones that followed soon after, that convinced me that I had to write this secret story.

In my mind's eye I see Tony, unshaven and shabbily dressed (he never showed much of an interest in clothes), in an under-furnished Connemara cottage, starting to write this letter several times, and then tearing up each version; forced by the circumstances to drop his usual circumlocutory mélange of reticence and jocularity.

Only in its closing lines does Tony slip in a playful remark – such a feature of all his other letters – and there is little reticence. The final version of the letter – five neat pages written in black ink, and kept by my father for more than fifty years – has no slips or crossings out, though the language he uses in the first paragraph is unusually nervous and unpolished.

15 October 1958   Cleggan

Connemara

EIRE

Dear Karlo,

I've hesitated before writing to you, because until today I wasn't sure how to write to you. First, I thought of saying I would dodge the issue, doing so, and ricocheting off into news and chit-chat. Then, I felt I mustn't dodge the issue, but must bare my thoughts to you. Today I made up my mind to do the second, as more fitting: so without further ado, here goes.

Once Tony decides not to 'dodge the issue', his writing becomes as fluent and as confident as ever, and he moves quickly to the crux of the matter.

I've no idea what you think of me at the moment, so it is hard to write in keeping with your mood, and I must chance it and write straight from the heart. You may be thinking me a complete and utter shit, you may just feel a mild sense of disappointment and disgust in me. I should like to think neither, but there is no reason to suppose so.

I won't insult you by any excuse – there are none. I knew exactly what I was doing, of course, and risked losing your good opinion and affection, a loss I can't bear to consider. A big risk, but I felt it would, in the final instance, work out all right.

It becomes clear from what follows that Tony and my father had discussed issues of fidelity before. And the letter then takes a more philosophical and theoretical turn, with an unexpected, and distinctly pre-feminist twist.

> You know, more or less, my attitude towards sex, and that I have an odd morality about it – which I think in senses is like yours and in other senses not. What it amounts to for present purposes is that I don't hold sexual fidelity very high. In concrete terms, I'd be pretty angry if my wife (or equivalent) slept with C—n, but delighted if she slept with you (as my friend). I know I wouldn't mind in the slightest: would, in fact, be happy in the knowledge. Don't for Christ's sake, think that I am using this as an excuse, nor do I presume (and what presumption it would be) you should think the same. On the other hand, if she showed a marked inclination to share her life with you rather than me, I'd be concerned because it would destroy the point of our being married or allied. Does this explain my conduct?

I find this passage rather astonishing, on first reading and now that I have pondered his words many times over. My father, I think, had a less theoretical view of infidelity than Tony, and, as will be seen, wasn't terribly interested in a Socratic dialogue on the subject. He would have said that infidelity was both common and unsurprising, and perhaps wisely stayed away from the ethical issues involved.

Tony, on the other hand, was keen to navigate his way through the fog and mud of moral uncertainty. And his solution, it seems, was to philosophise his relationship with the wife of one of his closest friends, as if it were a natural extension of that friendship.

He does finally give a qualified apology.

> I'm not sorry for what I've done, but I am most, most sorry if
> what I've done has hurt you – and unless you share my views
> (which I doubt) it must have. The purpose of this letter is to
> hope most fervently that you'll not let such hurt jaundice our
> friendship, as it is one of the very few things that matters to
> me, and binds me to London and England – and makes me
> regret being here.
>
> One thing I must say: my actions were at no time born of
> calculation, only of impulse. I hope you believe that, and see
> it's important. It is to me.
>
> Please write me what you truly feel. I'd rather you told
> me to fuck off out of your life, than have me on sufferance.
> Till I know, I can't falsify and write you news-items or even
> go on with this letter.

And he ends the letter with what could almost be seen as a love
message to my father, an impassioned plea for their friendship to
continue. He returns to the gentle teasing of old, with an ironic
reference to my father's legendary sense of irony, and by signing off
with his newly coined nickname.

> Even if you never wish to see me more – know that nothing
> could anger me further than that anyone should slight you,
> or run you down, and my affection and admiration for you,
> I have never concealed, nor ever will. It's one of the few con-
> stants. If I've not made this clear to you before, it's because the

time wasn't right: now it is, and you can drive the long thin steel of irony, if you will, through my protestations.

Yours,

Testa d'Oro

Finally there is a little postscript, one that seemed likely to complicate matters still further.

I enclose a note for Jane that she's at liberty to show you if she wants

That note has also survived, kept separately for more than half a century by my mother. She thought she hadn't kept it, but recently it reappeared. The other day, she came clutching it in her hand, and shyly put it next to me on my father's desk where I was writing.

The note to my mother, that she was 'at liberty' to show my father was a companion piece to the main letter, originally nestled inside the same envelope. It begins baldly, with my mother's name – and quickly asserts how important both of them are to him. Tony seems to be saying that unless he is forgiven he will cast himself into exile.

Jane,

Please forgive me for any hurt I've done to you or Karl, or to both of you jointly. I hate to think of it: and hope terribly it's not great or lasting. I am so dependent on your loves, that to lose one or both, would leave me little appetite ever to return to England again – especially after this summer with you both.

The next paragraph resurrects the notion of envy from the pre-lapsarian letters to my father, as a way of praising my mother. But the latter part is obscure – and I am not sure what he means when he says 'I must do the same myself'. Was he saying that he meant to get married himself? It seems out of character.

> I can't now say anything more personal to you which would be adequate: save that my fondness for you has made me see most clearly why Karl married you before you went away and were out of his sphere – and I envy him that. And that I must do the same myself. This compliment is so indirect it scarcely merits the name: but it is one, and meant.

He's unwilling to let go of my mother entirely, though. He requests, even expects, her to retain something of her affection for him – in, remember, a letter which he intended that my father would also read.

> Love Karl, as he deserves, but keep a corner of affection for me, and be tolerant of this poor letter

> Testa d'Oro

108

Both of these letters, once companions in the same envelope, hold out the possibility of Tony White removing himself from my parents' life – indeed of going into voluntary exile, like the hero of some Romantic play, or Sir Lancelot again, perhaps. And so he sat in Connemara awaiting some kind of decision from my father.

My father was slow to respond, taking well over a month to write to Tony. His letter does not survive. That is a sadness to me, largely because I know how elegantly written it would have been, and because I would have enjoyed parsing it for his irony and his circumlocutions. But it is possible to work out what he said from Tony's next letter – which is full of football-obsessed bounciness, and, more than anything, relief that my father seemed to have forgiven him.

5th December   Cleggan
Connemara
EIRE

Dear Karl,

I must write at once and tell you how glad I was to have your letter and know you had not banished me [to] the suburbs of your pleasure. I totally agree with you about limiting talk to the minimum, and feel we should devote ourselves to more positive ends, such as selecting teams.

Much of the rest of the letter is devoted to his forthcoming visit to London – and their football plans. He suggests names, many of them old friends from Cambridge, who might play in the team – but asks my father to make the final selection. He returns to the theme of his previous letter by saying that when he appears in ten days or so, 'I will present you my throat to be cut.' And ends the letter by admitting that,

I was afraid you had thought bad things of me and I'd not know what to do on return, so I'm overjoyed you wrote.

My love to you, Jane and Daniel.
T. d'Oro

This, then, was the end of the matter – for now. My father had decreed there should be no more discussion of the affair, and that Tony and he should revert to the far more important business of being joint player-managers of Battersea Park football team.

I can find no evidence that any of the three, Karl, Jane or Tony, spoke to anyone else about what had happened. And they did not discuss it again among themselves.

109

Tony did write at great length about the holiday in Italy to their old Cambridge friend Thom Gunn, now living in America, but omitted the affair. Instead, Tony recounted how he and my father read Gibbon's *Decline and Fall of the Roman Empire* to each other, and then switched to singing nursery rhymes and obscene songs in descant. He did refer to Karl's jealousy, but only when he described how Italian men leered at 'Jane's long, inciting tresses'.

And he explained, as if it might need some explanation, that he had only stayed on after Karl had left because Sasha had wanted someone who could drive them around in Sicily. He described how much he loved his time in Sicily, and the most excited part of the letter is about a visit he made to a village with my mother. He tells Thom that he would like to live in Sicily for a while, and 'would return there at a moment's notice'.

When Tony travelled back to London from Connemara in mid-December 1958 he was accepted back into my parents' circle of close friends, and into the heart of their busy lives. His relationship with them returned, ostensibly, to what it had been before the Roman holiday.

On arrival, he spent two successive evenings at my parents' flat – though there were others present on both occasions. Tony and my father played football together again. And then he came to dinner alone with the two of them, on successive Saturdays, before returning to Ireland and the lobster farm at the end of January.

The three of them even began to plan another summer holiday together – my parents and brother visiting Tony in his Irish isolation this time. It didn't happen, partly because my parents took fright at Tony's description of quite how primitive living conditions were on the island where he was staying. He may have been trying to scare them off.

III

On his return to Ireland, Tony attempted to reinvent himself as a full-time writer. If was as if he was now more certain about what he wanted to do with his life. He began work almost simultaneously on a novel, a short story and a TV play – and he also, sporadically, wrote a journal, parts of which survive. His old friend, John Holmstrom agreed to act as his agent, and Tony asked him not to tell any of their acquaintances of his plans. He wanted to surprise them with his success – or perhaps not to have to deal with the public humiliation of any failure.

In the inaugural 1959 entry in his journal, he reflects briefly and pointedly on how my parents had conducted themselves towards him in London: 'Karl was magnificent, burningly enthusiastic about football and full of healing towards me: though I noted the odd moment of "nostalgia" in Jane.'

112

In 1960, my mother and Tony would resume their affair with, for me, rather important consequences.

2014:5

My father did not die in 'a matter of weeks'.

Indeed, at the end of that seven-week period I had marked in my diary he was much stronger than at the start. He remained very ill, though, and the clear shape of his pacemaker remained visible through the skin of his chest. But he had begun to eat with gusto; and he took it upon himself to entertain us, often as wisely as Lear's Fool.

He still slept a lot, and unpredictably – and some unlucky visitors would find him semi-comatose, and leave thinking this was indubitably a dying man. But at other times he sparkled brilliantly, and in a way that was more unguarded than in the past. He was less embarrassed, perhaps, than he would once have been, by winsome words of endearment exchanged with his family.

The showpiece event of our new daily routine was an eleven o'clock coffee meeting in his bedroom with my brother and me. It was then that we came to be known, as if we were members of some ancient and clandestine gentlemen's drinking club, as 'The Shitehawks'. My father would take some time to get himself ready. If he felt too weak or lazy to go to the bathroom he would piss in a bucket by his bed ('Avert your beautiful eyes,' he would say, and then, 'Talk brilliantly among yourselves'). We would bring him coffee, milky and sweet, which he always declared to be 'wonderful', and two chocolate digestive biscuits.

One Shitehawk morning, flicking through an anthology of Scottish poetry I chanced upon 'The Tryst', by William Soutar, which I read to my father, and it brought him close to tears and led to a flood of teenage nostalgia. He had not read the poem since he was at school. The poem, he said, described his favourite fantasy, the yearnings of his youth, in what he referred to as his 'pre-carnal' days: it was a poem about a young man who is visited in his bed by a woman (her breists sae sma' and roun') – and they say not a word, but make love all night, their entangled limbs never separating.

A' thru the nicht we spak nae word
Nor sinder'd bane frae bane:

'I couldnae dae any o' that now,' he lamented, switching to the language of his childhood and leaning back on his bed with a wistful smile.

On another memorable Shitehawk morning he became a performer, as if he were a veteran of the music hall. He decided first that I should replace him on the bed, and he sat on the chair. I began taking a video of him, and he complained about how hard this made it for him to be 'spontaneous'.

'Spontaneous! You heard of that word?' he said to me with the feigned harshness that we all knew well, but which could terrify the uninitiated.

He then picked up an old toilet roll, and announced, apropos of nothing, 'Scipio Africanus takes the stage', and proceeded to use the toilet roll as a rudimentary trumpet, ending his musical interlude from the works of Handel with a loud farting noise.

We two brothers are both laughing, audibly, off-screen on the video tape. My father looked pleased with himself, and informed us gravely that he had 'always been good at grace notes'. I said I wasn't quite sure what a grace note was. He explained with a delicate segue into the Scottish ballad 'Leezie Lindsay', which he peppered with some extra little vocal sound effects, grace notes no doubt, to express his individual approach to the art of singing. He hadn't yet invented 'Rufty McTufty', but he did dream up a new line for the ballad. 'Your kilt,' he sang, 'it is far too short, Sir,' providing Leezie with yet another reason for not following Lord Ronald McDonald to the Highlands.

He then turned to me and said he didn't want to be recorded any more 'because it cramps my style – I don't feel able to sing if someone is trailing a huge camera up my armpit.' I pretended to turn it off.

And then he turned to my brother, Daniel, usually more silent and thoughtful than me at these moments. 'Daniel's had enough. He's looking at his watch, for Chrissakes. We're having a lovely time.'

Daniel denied he was looking at his watch, and agreed that we were having the time of our lives. On other occasions he would be taken to task for just the slightest suspicion of a yawn.

My father's bravura performance continued.

Father: I'm rather aggressive as a father, don't you think?

Me: You're quite funny.

Father: Yes, but I tend to insist we talk about X rather than Y, things like that.

A few seconds' silence.

Me: Naughty Kiteman?

Father: Cow pats?

His hearing was not very good, but sometimes he would play his deafness for laughs. I wanted him to sing my favourite of all his made-up songs, the Naughty Kiteman, composed for the occasion on which my brother declared that someone had done 'cacac', our childhood word for shit, in his kite. He spoke it out loud first, and then sang it to us, when I insisted, complete with grace notes.

Is it true that the Naughty Kiteman
Did cacac in his kite?
Did he creep late at night in the park and
Relieve himself there out of sight?
Oh no, that very fine Kiteman,
No friend of the alfresco pee,
Would never have crept in the park
And relieved himself there privily

'That's the whole thong,' my father declared at the end, referencing my childhood lisp.

Soon the phone rang, and I put my camera down, and the Shitehawk session was over. The whole wonderful, mad sequence from Scipio Africanus on the toilet roll to the Naughty Kiteman lasted less than seven minutes.

He was, briefly, in one of those footballing clichés that he thought so funny, at the top of his game.

113

There's a feral honeysuckle plant in the small L-shaped garden behind my parents' home in Chelsea. It's older than I am, but has lost none of its vigour. As I sit now at my father's desk, looking out of the window, the honeysuckle is slowly and gently strangling a rose bush, and its long, cascading tresses have overflowed into the neighbour's garden.

As a child, I used to pluck the honeysuckle's yellow, tubular flowers, then gently peel back the petals, and, like a bumble bee, dip my tongue into the faux-honey that collects at the base. Recently, I learned from my mother that the honeysuckle had been grown from a cutting taken by Tony White from his parents' home in Notting Hill. It was a housewarming gift, presented when my parents moved into Limerston Street in the summer of 1960.

Relations between Tony and my parents had found a new equilibrium after the Italian holiday. He remained a close friend and footballing colleague of my father, and he was rarely, if ever, alone with my mother – but was very much a regular visitor to their flat. He told them less about his life than he used to; and they were unaware, for instance, of his struggles to become a writer.

Tony spent much of 1959 away from their London world – in Ireland, where my parents believed he was simply living out a romantic, bucolic dream of being a fisherman and a lobster farmer living in a remote rural community. In fact, he was writing. It was a tough year for Tony, and as he was turning thirty in early 1960, he described his life, in a letter to Thom Gunn, as 'a fuck-up'.

While in Ireland, Tony completed a TV play and a short story, and started on a novel. But he soon lost confidence in his abilities as a writer, telling Thom

> I am still tinkering [with] my novel, but never had a man less talent than I for words. I don't know how I have the nerve to continue, but a horse in blinkers will try anything. Maybe I can thrash it into some pattern by the summer, at present it's as shapely and appetising as cold rice-pudding (which actually I am quite fond of, so even my metaphors are inept).

These writings were not a success: the TV play was never performed, and the short story was never published. The novel was not completed. Rejection and self-doubt hit him hard. It's apparent from his letters and his journal that he found this a humiliation. After all, he had turned his back, decisively, on the theatre. He had been considered a great talent, and many of his friends were shocked that he should give up acting, which he described as mere 'posturing in fancy dress'.

He preferred the idea of being a writer – it was, in his view, a more genuine calling; but he was, perhaps, used to the immediate acclaim of the stage, and found it hard to deal with rejection. He had also run out of money.

The most obvious move would have been to return to acting – and he did lend his voice for audio recordings of several Shakespeare plays. But he could not bear the embarrassment of returning full-time to the profession he had scorned.

115

He retained his grand Romantic ideas; and talked still of his philosophy and his values, of doing something noble, of reconciling 'the worlds of ideas and action'. A quarter of a century earlier he might have gone off to fight in the Spanish Civil War – but Tony White never found his cause. He told his friends that he was thinking of joining the Irish army, which was providing peacekeepers to the United Nations in Congo, or of becoming an explorer.

In fact, he continued to survive on a number of part-time jobs, as he alternated between Connemara and London. He did find lots of short-term work, of a kind his Cambridge friends would never do. He drove a London delivery van full of dirty nappies; worked for the North Thames Gas Board; picked grapes in Burgundy; helped convert a trawler into a yacht; managed a small garage in Chelsea; and continued to work at the Connemara lobster farm.

And my mother steered some other kind of work his way – she was working for a publishing company three days a week and recommended Tony as a reader, and before long he was translating books from French.

I was more than surprised when I first read Tony White's diary entry for March 1960. So surprised that I immediately reached for my phone to call my mother.

Tony had written: 'The Millers are buying a house and have offered me a flat there, which I must take.' This seemed most unlikely, given what had happened in Rome a year and a half earlier. It was true that my parents were buying a house then, the one they would live in together for more than half a century – and that they had a series of lodgers who stayed in one of the basement rooms. My mother has no recollection of any suggestion that Tony might live in Limerston Street, and it seems unlikely that she would forget such an idea, given the circumstances.

This offer can only have come as a suggestion from my father that was never discussed with my mother. I came across the diary after my father died, so I can but guess at his version. Perhaps Tony misheard him, perhaps mistook a passing thought or a gesture of friendship for a definite proposal, perhaps my father had forgotten all about what happened in Rome, or maybe he hadn't and still liked the notion of the three of them living together. I don't know.

Tony never stayed at Limerston Street but he did help my parents move into their new home. Not only did he provide the garden with one of its first plants, but he helped my mother paint the kitchen. And it's at about that time that their affair resumed.

I've struggled to reconstruct the timeline of the summer of 1960 – with only diary entries and my mother's memory to rely on. She can't remember the specific order of events and Tony himself is unmentioned, deliberately, in her appointment diaries. This might not matter, but I am keen to know whether the relationship between my mother and Tony restarted before or after Tony and my father went on a walking holiday together.

My mother, after looking at her diaries, thinks the relationship resumed when my father went to Scotland in early July, with my brother, to visit his aunts. According to those diaries, my mother was painting the house at that time (there is a mention of Sasha coming over to help her paint). And she remembers, clearly, Tony and her together, painting in the kitchen, and that their second affair began then and there.

But, and this is why the timeline is of interest to me, just ten days after my father returns from Edinburgh, he goes on a walking holiday in Wales with Tony. My mother does not remember this sequence of events – which seems unlikely if her lover and her husband were having a holiday together. My father later recalled this holiday with a mixture of pain and pleasure, in the form of blisters and beer, and he spoke fondly of Tony's companionship and inexhaustibility.

Maybe my interest in this level of detail is a little unhealthy. But I would like to know if my father went on holiday with his closest friend, knowing that his friend and his wife were having an affair.

I don't know whether my father was having an affair at that time. He did have several affairs during their marriage of more than fifty years. Did this fact make him feel less jealous about my mother and Tony, or less guilty about his other relationships?

Undoubtedly, during different parts of the summer of 1960, Tony spent a lot of time alone with both my father and my mother. And, in November, he notes in his journal

> I've earned some money, been to Ireland for six weeks, had holidays in Wales [with Karl Miller] and Cornwall, had a renewed affair with Jane. Life has been rich and almost seems to be marching towards some goal.

The affair carried on for nine months. Neither my mother nor Tony talked about it with my father, but she is clear that he knew about their relationship.

Tony and my mother would meet once a week, usually on a Friday, at Tony's flat in Notting Hill. She remembers that he had a TV, and that they'd always watch *Coronation Street*, which started in December 1960 – now the world's longest running television soap opera. Tony admired the acting, and the way that it portrayed working-class life realistically.

My mother is a *Coronation Street* devotee to this day. My father wasn't a fan for many decades, considering it a nostalgic travesty of working-class life, but in his later more nostalgic years he became a regular viewer.

In 1960, my parents held a Christmas party at their new home in Limerston Street. More than forty black-and-white photographs of this party survive, most of them retrieved by me from a huge, neglected hoard of photos squirrelled away by my mother in an old desk, and several more kept by my father in a shoebox at the foot of his bed. No one seems to be able to remember who the photographer was.

These are photos I've scrutinised again and again, as if they were archaeological relics, helping me to make sense of my immediate prehistory, and of the world into which I, at the start of 1962, would be born. For me, they are interesting on several levels.

First, on a more technical level, they show the interior detail of the house in which I was born, and in which I am now writing these words. I'm amazed by how instantly familiar everything is, even in close-up. I know, almost intimately, every moulding, architrave and skirting board – and can spot immediately where minor changes were necessitated by the arrival of central heating in the 1980s. So much else has also survived: the old fireplaces, door handles, lamp stands, tables and chairs, even round-pin plug sockets. My parents did not believe in change for the sake of change.

Second, there are the keen, bright faces of grown-ups having a good time. I recognise many, younger than when I first knew them, without the jowls of middle age. I show them to my mother, and we talk about those who died young, or disappeared from my parents' lives.

And then there is the mystery of the photographer, and why he, or she, took these particular photos – for some of them seem almost to betray a knowledge of the secrets of those portrayed.

Most of all, these photos seem to capture a key moment in the complex lives of the three principal actors in this story.

123

My father appears in eight of the photos, though I can spot his striped trousers intruding into several more. Karl Miller looks entirely relaxed, with a broad smile on his face, and a cigar in his hand. In two of them he looks straight back, almost flirtatiously, at the photographer, as if to ask why the camera had been allowed to interrupt their conversation.

My father is twenty-nine, and to use that footballing analogy again, at the top of his game; charming and funny, with a fine line in irony and self-deprecation – and it's possible for me, looking at these photos, almost to feel that I was there, and that I remember him like this.

124

My mother has just turned twenty-eight. She is long-haired and radiant, and appears in more than half of the photos. She is never with my father, though I think it would be a mistake for me to read anything into this. She's wearing a patterned skirt with a slit up the side – her home-made dancing skirt. And in more than half the photos she is dancing (and my mother would carry on dancing until her knees wore out in her sixties). She is showing everyone just how high she can kick her legs, and just how well she can shimmy her way across what I would later know as the TV room. She is unaware of the camera but conscious that she has a live audience.

There are two male dancing partners with her in the photographs: one of them, with whom she does high kicks, I do not recognise. The other is Tony White, whose dancing style is a little less competitive, and more chivalrous, more ballroom, in a way that involves the touching of hands.

Then there is another group of photos from later in the evening: here my mother looks a little tired, perhaps tipsy – as if all that dancing has taken its toll. She has a cocktail umbrella in her hair and is sitting silently on the arm of a sofa.

Seated on the actual sofa, just below her, is Tony White.

125

There are a total of twelve photos in which Tony appears. He is about to turn thirty-one, and is of no fixed employment or abode. These are the only adult images of him that I have come across in which he wears a tie, and in most of the photos he appears to be nervous and camera-shy.

There's one attempted portrait of him alone on the sofa: his eyes are closed, and the whiteness of the flash has turned him into something of a ghost. One hand is raised as if he were about to cover his face. In the others, dancing with my mother, he is unaware of the camera. He is attentive to her, looking her in the eye, and holding out his hand, as if she is leading. Elsewhere, seated with others on the sofa, he's more comfortable – but listening, dreamily observing, not entirely engaged.

126

And there's a final photo that gave me a fright when I first saw it.

It shows my father looking squarely at the camera, and behind him, appearing over his right shoulder, in profile, is the top half of a man's head – his eyes looking down. And the reason this photo gave me such a fright is because the head in profile appears to be me, as a grown-up – some thirteen months before I was born. Of course, it's actually Tony, but it looks more like me than him. The upper parts of our faces are almost identical. And I just can't understand how more of my parents' friends did not guess I was Tony's son.

127

At the time of that Christmas Party, the affair between my mother and Tony still had many episodes of *Coronation Street*, and another five months, to run. In May 1961 she discovered that she was pregnant and decided to end the affair immediately. She told them both, Karl and Tony – and said that she couldn't be sure which of them was the father, but thought it was more likely to be Tony's. Separately, they both suggested that an abortion might be the best course of action. She says that neither of them pushed her on the issue, but made it clear that this was their preference.

Getting an abortion in the early 1960s was not a simple matter. It was il-
legal, unless it could be proven that the health of the mother was in danger.

On Monday 29 May 1961, my mother went to see a doctor, an abortionist by the name of Gross, whom a friend had recommended. This
doctor explained that he could not terminate her pregnancy unless
two other doctors agreed that an abortion was necessary in order to
safeguard her health. And in her case, he explained, since there was no
physical reason why she should not give birth, these doctors would
have to be psychiatrists. And they would have to attest that giving birth
would be a threat to her mental health. The uncertain paternity, he
felt, should provide sufficient psychological grounds for an abortion.
He provided her with the names of two psychiatrists, and she made ap-
pointments to see them on the Thursday and Friday of the same week.

The first psychiatrist, a Dr Rolls, had his clinic in Cadogan Gardens – a
short walk from my parents' home. My mother visited him at 4 p.m. on
1 June, according to her diary, in what would prove to be a decisive day
in my unborn life. She told him, baldly, what had happened. She said that
the two men were friends. That they ran a football team together. He
said, 'I think you're the football here.'

At that moment, my mother decided to go ahead with the pregnancy.

She cancelled the appointment with the second psychiatrist and she
told the two men in her life that she was not going to have an abortion.
Neither of them tried to convince her otherwise.

My father said that he would treat the child as his own. While Tony said that he would make no claim on the child. And that would be the basis on which I was brought up: as the son of Karl Miller. Of course, I can't quite believe it was so simple for these two men.

130

According to my father, the two men never spoke about the issue of my paternity. They exchanged letters, he said, before I was born. These do not survive – my father told me he destroyed the ones Tony wrote to him. And I've been unable to track down any of the letters either of my parents wrote to Tony.

It does, however, seem likely that the two men had discussed the issue of the abortion prior to my mother's decision to go ahead with the pregnancy. Just three days before my mother's appointment with the abortionist, my father's diary records that he and Tony met for lunch. I discovered this after my father's death and so was unable to ask him what they talked about. 'Football,' I think, would have been his answer.

131

Many mothers have considered abortion, or wished for an abortion and then gone ahead with having the child. I don't think I am unusual, except that I know about it.

A friend told me that I must be troubled by knowing that I was nearly aborted.

I said, 'I'm not, honestly'.

'Deep down,' she said.

'I don't think so,' I replied, 'but I suppose it is just about possible. Subconsciously.'

I was keen to end that conversation.

In all the hundreds of thousands of words of memoir and letter writing (probably millions of words, in fact) left behind by Karl Miller and Tony White, I have only found one reference to the issue of my paternity. It takes the form of a short, bland sentence in the penultimate entry in Tony's journal: 'a long-drawn out affair with Jane ended when she found she was pregnant, possibly by me.'

I think I would have been pleased if there was more than that.

It's clear from my parents' appointment diaries that they saw little of Tony in the summer of 1961– and since the abortive abortion happened towards the end of the football season, my father and Tony did not have immediate sporting reasons to spend much time together. But still they remained within each other's orbits; and the football season resumed in the autumn.

In 1961 there's a second Christmas party, with accompanying photographs, held just a few weeks before I was born. My mother is not dancing. Instead, she is sitting down, a cigarette in her hand, wearing a rather stylish home-made tent.

This time my father has dressed more traditionally, in a three-piece suit and striped tie, and seems to be having a whale of a time. Tony on the other hand has dressed down for the occasion, and appears to be dancing for England. He's taken off his jersey, and large sweaty shadows have appeared in his armpits. His shirt has become untucked to reveal a white vest beneath – and he's dancing and flirting with my mother's friend Pam.

136

Three weeks later, I was born in my mother's bedroom on the top floor of the Limerston Street house.

'BABY BORN 9 p.m.' my mother reported to her diary. It had been an easy labour. My mother had suggested to the midwife that my father be asked to boil some water. The midwife said, 'We don't actually need boiling water; we only say that to keep husbands out of the way. Yours is busy with his friends anyway.'

Downstairs, my father, Tony and their other football-loving friends were having a good time, and, perhaps, waiting for news of my arrival. My mother thinks only my father came up to see me. I was much larger and had more hair at birth than my older brother, and my skin was darker. My mother had no doubt that I was Tony's son.

My father continued to recover through the early summer of 2014. One fine day, when his friend Andy O'Hagan was coming over for lunch, he made his slow way down two flights of steps from his bedroom to the kitchen. I took a photo of my father in the kitchen on my mobile phone and sent it, uncaptioned, to my far-flung children – one in Lyon, the other in Delhi.

'When was that?' they responded, almost in unison, presuming it was before he had fallen ill.

The palliative care consultant walked over from the hospital twice more – suggesting on the first visit, to my visible and audible consternation, that he still only had a matter of weeks to live. I felt just a little vindicated when she withdrew that prediction on the subsequent visit. My father was able to quiz her by then:

> Father: How would you describe my state of health?
> Doctor: (after a long pause) Precarious.
> Father: Well, that's a good word but a pretty poor state of affairs.

In late May, my father left the house for the first time in more than three months, a wheelchair trip to the river, just a short walk from our home. We all loved it, but he was in agony. His frailty and scrawniness meant that he felt every crack in the paving, every irregularity of the kerbstones, and the rim of every manhole cover as if he were on some fairground rollercoaster. We children, each in our fifties, competed over our wheelchair-pushing skills. He chose me as the best, 'the smoothest', and I was delighted, the only non-driver of us three.

We all sat in a park overlooking the Thames, discussing how the skyline on the Battersea side of the river had changed over the last half century. Only the Old Church, where William Blake was married, and from where Turner painted, was left. I took photos of us and posted one of them – a selfie plus parents – on Facebook. It was my way of telling my friends, particularly those whom I had left in India, that things were getting better. It received more likes and comments than anything I'd ever put up on Facebook. I was feeling very pleased with myself.

But now, when I look at that photograph I feel something rather different. I see me, self-satisfied, larger than life, with a huge grin; my mother leaning back, exhausted, soaking up the sun; and a bewildered sadness to my shrunken father, blinded by the light, his glasses now far too large for his emaciated face. He was not enjoying himself. And I was behaving, triumphantly, as if it was I,

not he, who had been battling his illness. I had put away, in the recesses of my mind, the suicide conversation – and was on a high, imagining the future milestones of my father's survival. He would surely carry on, until my children returned, until the World Cup started, until his birthday in August, into the autumn and winter – indefinitely, for ever.

My father began to make more journeys outside, usually with a lot of help from wheelchairs and taxis and his family, particularly those who could drive. There was a grim determination to him. He hated to miss an appointment – even the most routine one – especially if it was medical, and it had already been written into his diary. And so he had his pacemaker checked, his hearing aid tested, his teeth examined. He walked as far as Luigi's, his favourite delicatessen, where they greeted him with cheers and chocolate, and a chair made out of cardboard boxes for him to rest on. He went to a family party, a lunch, a private view and a birthday dinner – and joined in, though it always seemed an effort.

He was able once again to read and comment wisely, and did so – sometimes witheringly – on an article I had written about Gandhi in London. He began to watch the news again, and *Coronation Street*. He'd look at the *Guardian* each morning, and pull books out of his shelves, but he never really enjoyed reading prose as he had before; though poetry could still hold him spellbound.

My children soon returned and spent many happy hours with him, as did his other grandchildren. He watched the football World Cup with my son, but without the all-consuming pleasure he once took from the game. His opinions were as incisive and as dismissive of mine as usual but, honestly, he'd lost interest. Books and football, these mainstays of his life, had faded into unimportance.

In July, I decided he was well enough for me to go away for a bit; I wrote to a friend that 'I don't feel I need to be here any more'. I wanted to wander, as always, and got a short-term BBC job, in Nigeria – a new country for me. My father was not happy with me for leaving, and told me so. But he improved while I was away, his cheeks swelled and reddened, and he had more energy. I returned briefly for his birthday, on 2 August, where he assumed responsibility for entertaining us all, as of old, family and friends, at a gathering at Limerston Street – and he and I competed with each other to eat as many smoked mussels as possible. I returned properly to London in mid-August 2014, for – and I would never have guessed it then – what turned out to be the final month of his life.

PART THREE

137

If this were fiction, the period immediately after my birth would have been the climax of my story; a 'tug-of-war' perhaps, or an act of desertion. This was not the case.

138

In 1962 there was no meltdown, no eruption, no terrible moment of truth; there was not even a marital crisis. Instead, a lot of nappies were changed, and a fat-cheeked, greedy baby drank abnormal quantities of milk. The plain biological facts of my paternity were kept secret. Once again, the three principal actors in this story each got on with their lives, now more entangled than ever, but they behaved as if nothing unusual had happened.

As I write about these events now, more than half a century later, I am almost disappointed. I shouldn't be – it would have made my life a lot more complicated, but it would, I suppose, have made this a more dramatic story. But the drama, I have come to realise, is in the detail – and it is there, of course, in the early death of Tony White.

139

In the years after I was born, Tony White visited Limerston Street slightly less often – and probably saw little of me. He'd be there at parties, or to watch football on TV, but he wouldn't drop by uninvited.

Two months after my birth he sent my parents a postcard with what was, by his standards, a humdrum message – about a holiday in the Camargue – and he signs off, 'Love to Daniel and Sam. Tony.' That's one of only two references to me that appear in all of Tony's surviving letters and other writings. (The second reference, written just two months before he died, would prove more significant, to me at least.) The rest of the correspondence from this period may have never existed, or has been lost or destroyed. Nothing has survived between Tony or either of my parents for a period of five years. So I have had to rely largely on my mother's formidable memory. There are some other clues, though.

140

Recently I tracked down an old girlfriend of Tony's, another secret married lover, who took me to lunch in a pub near Brighton. She had kept his small appointment diary for 1963: the year after I was born, the same year they became lovers, and she gave it to me.

I already had appointment diaries for my father and mother and so by triangulating the events to which they refer, I have a small idea, a snapshot, of how they navigated their way, wordlessly, through their entangled relationship.

Tony came over to the house at least three times in 1963 – for a dinner, for a party, and to watch the FA Cup Final on TV with my father. There were other outside occasions at which all three of them were together, but my mother and Tony did not meet alone. However, Tony and my father continued to spend a great deal of time in each other's company. They went to football matches together (watching England, Chelsea and Spurs all play at home in the autumn of 1963), and, of course, they continued to play for the same team on Sunday mornings. And my mother would sometimes turn up with her two little boys to watch their fathers playing football in the park.

141

Many of Battersea Park football club's teamsheets also survive, in Tony's handwriting. And Tony's and Karl's names – White and Miller – are often paired next to each other in attack: my father as inside right, Tony as centre-forward. As they got older they both crept back down the pitch into defence.

There are also dozens of formal team photos, two stilted rows of intellectual footballers. In one of the team photos, with Tony and Karl on either side of the goalkeeper, they are wearing white shirts bearing the four-towered silhouette of Battersea Power Station – an act, I later discovered, of modest defiance. For also in the football scrapbook is a letter to Tony, who has been told, with wonderful pomposity, by the Regional Public Relations Officer for the Central Electricity Generation Board, that under no circumstances would the team be allowed to use an image of the power station on their shirts.

142

There's another photo, though, that is special to me. My favourite picture of Tony and Karl. It's the first photo I find myself showing to those few people to whom I have told this story.

I think I like it so much because it was taken not long after my birth, and these two men – my two fathers, I suppose – seem so inordinately happy together. That, frankly, is a relief to me. At times, I somehow guiltily imagine them just about putting up with each other in the cause of familial and sporting harmony. But it's a photo that reassures me of something that, at heart, I know – that they were very fond of each other, and remained so, despite all that had happened, despite me.

In this photo, they are both in a state of partial undress, changing into their football gear in Battersea Park – and laughing. And the photographer has caught them with almost identical broad, natural smiles on their faces, captured as they face the camera, but looking down at something that they found funny. There must have been some joke, perhaps about the upside-down manner in which Tony, seated on the ground, is putting on his socks. Whatever it was they are totally at ease with one another. Despite my existence they can remain great friends. And perhaps, and I accept that this may be foolish and wishful thinking on my part, it may even have brought them closer. It's not a line that I can support with evidence. But I suppose it reflects a later anxiety on my part about the effect I might have had on these two men's lives.

In early June 1963, the football team went on tour to France, and Tony later pasted his account of the trip in the Battersea Park FC scrap album. There he recounted how the intrepid Londoners, playing against the semi-professionals of Fresnes, bounced back from a seven-goal deficit at half-time to score four of their own – losing 7–4 at the final whistle.

In his more general remarks about the trip he takes gentle aim at my father: 'Everyone seemed to enjoy the tour, especially Karl Miller, who got very pissed on the way back, smoked a lot of thin cigars and didn't even mind losing a lot of money at poker.'

My father would wait thirty years to get his own back. In his memoirs, he describes how Tony, leading the Battersea team out onto the playing fields of Fresnes, stumbled and fell, sprawling to the ground in front of their bemused opponents. Or as my father expressed it in Karlian English: 'Our captain, Tony, tripped over a sod and measured his length.'

My father doesn't only tease. He declares that after the match Francophone Tony gave an 'elegant speech of thanks' in Fresnes town hall. And it's part of a long, moving tribute to his friend's footballing persona: 'Tony was big and strong and eager, for ever being cut and gashed... His rich dark eyes, boundless generosity and zest, and his lavish brushstrokes on the field of play, held us together.' I read this passage out loud to my father not long before he died. If he had been writing about anyone else I would have teased my father about its homoerotic undertones.

Their friend and fellow footballer John Moynihan dedicated his book about park football to, among others, Karl Miller and Tony White. And inside the book, for the purposes of literature, Tony is transformed into Tiny Black, who on the field of play resembles an 'out-of-control Tiger tank'. As the years passed, Tony became more and more obsessed with playing football, while my father hung up his boots in 1972, not long after being told that he had all the qualities of a good footballer 'except speed and heart'.

He would not be a witness to the footballing incident at the end of 1975 which cost Tony his life.

144

I've just discovered a letter from my father to my mother dated 13 October 1963. She has gone to America to visit her sister. My father is in charge of us boys, with the help of an au pair. I am one and a half. The letter gives a small insight into the relationship between my parents after my birth.

> Dear Lovely Jane,
>
> I burn the midnight oil in my stinking study hoping you are having the best of times with Rachel and Jonathan – to whom my love. Nothing much has happened since you flew into the sun in your huge plane. Nappies have been deployed. Both boys are happy despite colds, which I don't think disturb them too much... [Daniel] sends you this nice drawing and his love. I send mine and Sammy's, who has been calling for you but not worryingly.
>
> Love, Karl

One more event that needs to be mentioned. My sister Georgia was born in early 1964. When I have told people this story, they seem particularly intrigued by the fact that I am a middle child – that both my older and younger siblings have Karl Miller as their biological father, and that I don't.

There are very few family photographs from the mid-sixties. And only one that shows my father with his three children. I found it very embarrassing as a youngster and destroyed at least one copy.

146

In the years after my birth, my mother and Tony saw less of each other, and were rarely alone, but their lives continued to intersect – and not just at football matches.

In the late fifties, my mother had introduced Tony to some of her colleagues in publishing. And in the early sixties, they were both reading French-language books for British publishers who were considering getting them translated into English. And on at least one occasion they both read the same book for the same publisher. There's a 1963 letter from Heinemann that I found recently in a pile of my mother's papers. It thanks my mother for a favourable review of a book by the Cameroonian novelist Ferdinand Oyono, and ends with the words, 'Tony White likes it too, so probably we shall do it.' She can't remember whether they had discussed the book.

147

Tony and my mother also both worked as actual translators, though my mother produced just one book, a memoir by a girlfriend of Picasso. She didn't enjoy translating. But Tony did. He translated at least seventeen books from French between 1961 and 1973 – including two Inspector Maigret stories by Simenon, several books about the Second World War, and a volume of memoirs by one of his earliest heroes, Jean-Paul Sartre. The latter was never published for reasons that are unclear, though it exists in galley form. My mother recalls that this was a disappointment to him, and may have been caused by the intervention of Sartre himself.

148

My French has never been as good as Tony's – or my mother's. But recently I began an experiment. I read the original French version of the Maigret stories alongside Tony's translations. I suppose I thought I should read everything Tony wrote, even translations, in the hope that it might help me understand Tony a little better. I don't think it really helped me do this, at least not in a way that is obvious to me.

But there has been a different, unexpected consequence of my experiment. I too have become a translator.

In the year after my father died, I spent four months working in Tunisia, a country where good French is essential. And, as a way of improving my French, I began to translate a nineteenth-century adventure story set in India, and now it is going to be published. There is something new and puzzling, in a way that appeals to me, about the act of translation. I feel for the first time that I am intimate with a text that isn't my own. I also hope it will mean more readers for a text that I love. Tony may have felt the same way about the Sartre translation.

149

By the mid-1960s Tony had become a jobbing writer – collaborating with a friend, Martin Green, on three editions of a guide to the pubs of London, and producing one book on his own, the long-forgotten *How to Run a Pub: Advice to Would-be Publicans*. He was also the ghost writer for *Contempt of Court*, the autobiography of Britain's most famous post-war jail-breaker, Alfie Hinds.

And that wasn't all. He seemed to take delight in trying out as many different jobs as possible: organising a poetry tour, working as a boathand, a fibreglass model-maker, a steel-fixer and, latterly, as a builder and handyman. By the late sixties, he would be called in by all his old Cambridge friends when they needed their roofs patched up, or their houses painted.

150

Tony settled into a life unlike those of his contemporaries. He had no permanent job or home; he moved every few months between Ireland and London. He had many dozens of adoring friends, and several lovers – often at the same time. Those who knew him first in the sixties repeat phrases like 'happy-go-lucky', 'larger-than-life', 'a wonderful friend', 'a private man', 'a great listener' to describe Tony. And it sometimes seems hard to get beyond the platitudes.

Very few of Tony's letters have survived from this period – and in those that do there is little sense of the inner turmoil that had caused him so much anguish and self-doubt in the fifties and early sixties. Those feelings may still have been there, but if so he concealed them from everyone.

He also stopped writing his diary. His sad last entry was written a month to the day before I was born. He lists his old friends and their successes, and compares himself to them:

Friends prosper. Karl has become Literary Editor of the *New Statesman*, Coleman film critic and Holmstrom dramatic critic. Nepotism! Who is as barren and destructive as myself? Not Michie, Director of Heinemann's, or Wood, big TV producer.

He concludes his final entry with the words,

I'll soon be 32. Not that it worries me, but six years have now gone by almost and what have I achieved? Fuck all.

My impending arrival is unmentioned, but I am left wondering whether it casts a shadow.

151

I do not know what my birth meant to Tony. But, occasionally, I imagine it helping him to reconcile himself with the world, to lower his expectations, to calm down, to stop imagining himself as a man of destiny. It's clear from his letters that he appeared less concerned by achievement in the years that followed my birth, and more intent on enjoying himself, and having an interesting life. Thirty years later, fatherhood – in rather different circumstances – would have such an impact on me.

Tony could not devote himself to fatherhood, and may not have wished to anyway, but instead he seems to have devoted himself to friendship – in a way that would make people dependent on his warmth and humour and good counsel. And he no longer burdened others with his own woes.

152

Tony loved playing the role of muse and editor to poets: principally his old Cambridge comrade Thom Gunn, and the Irish poet Richard Murphy – both of whom would reflect in verse on their friendship with Tony.

Richard Murphy met Tony on the quayside of Inishbofin in 1959 – and in 1974, two years before Tony's death, published an extremely short poem, 'Double Negative', which captured that moment

> You were standing on the quay
> Wondering who was the stranger on the mailboat
> While I was on the mailboat
> Wondering who was the stranger on the quay.

The poem, written in 1971, was originally more than ten times as long, and full of detailed biography: describing Tony as a Cambridge god, an Old Vic actor, a London lamp-lighter and a lobster fisherman. Richard Murphy showed Tony the original 55-line poem, as he did with all his work, and Tony was appalled. Richard noted in his diary that Tony said, quite firmly, 'there's a poem in the first four lines, but not in the rest.' This may have been a matter of literary judgement, but embarrassment may also have played its part.

This was Tony's chance to edit his biography, and he preferred to erase it, leaving behind just a four-line shadow. The other lines, struck through by Tony, were left to moulder in Richard's notebooks, including this final sequence which deals with Tony and friendship.

> We all believed we knew you well,
> each one you spoke to felt it was your soul
> that had something to say to his alone.
> You never did abuse this gift for gain,
> and then I wondered how much it cost you,
> creating this illusion
> in the mind of everyone to whom you spoke
> that he was somebody for whom you cared,

that spark, which was his true identity,

you struck alight, and held cupped in your hands

before the winds of boredom blew it out.

There's a suggestion here that Tony not only wanted to befriend everyone he met (and that may have irritated his existing friends such as Richard), but additionally that this almost ideological commitment to friendship involved some kind of subconscious self-control on Tony's part, a sublimation of his own needs.

153

Elsewhere, in a diary entry for 1967, Richard writes, 'Tony's needs are hidden from his closest friends: are they hidden from himself?'

154

Another poet friend, Ted Hughes, told Richard Murphy: 'Tony is someone who knows exactly what he is doing, who works hard and lives cheaply, and is free... Tony does not exhibit his doubts as some of his friends do, and with his friends he makes an effort to appear free of doubt, largely out of compassion.'

These speculations by his friends are a reminder that Tony remained something of a mystery even to those who knew him well. And neither Ted Hughes nor Richard Murphy were close to Tony in those days when he did declare his self-doubt to his friends, when he was prone to anguish, and, perhaps, to depression.

The nearest I can come to finding out what Tony really felt by the mid-sixties is a letter to Thom Gunn, whom he had known since 1951. Written in 1966, Tony accepts that he has changed, that he has lost his sense of ambition, which he'd anyway concealed from many of his friends.

> I'm as hopelessly unresolved as ever about my role in life and can't see more than a week ahead at a time. Or daren't... My life is a steady unambitious drift towards middle age. But what's the alternative? The romantic gestures sound hollow today. Material gain, the major alternative, God knows I don't despise, but it depresses me. Fame bores (and eludes) me. Yet I must say I'm very happy. Well, I suppose one should ask no more.

In the rest of this long, long letter to Thom, Tony talks of his love of the lyrics of 'Eleanor Rigby', his dislike of London life, and his wish to spend more time in Ireland. But he also talks of my father, with fondness ('old Karl'), and as the butt of his latest joke.

He explains to Thom that he has sent my father a letter, which he describes as 'a small ironical masterpiece'. It's a letter that I found in my father's papers, and it's hard to disagree with Tony's description.

The background: my parents had sent a taciturn young American, the son of a good friend, to visit Tony on the west coast of Ireland. The

young American had been uncommunicative to the point of rudeness –
and you did need to be very rude to offend Tony. And Tony then wrote
to my father:

Dear Karl,

How very thoughtful of you to send me your nice American friend. I always enjoy being tracked down in my little
hideaway here, even if I sometimes pretend not to. And I
do appreciate any link with the Old Country, even through
someone from a comparatively new country. However, I'm
afraid some misunderstanding may have arisen between us,
because when I asked your friend some rather innocuous
question... he seemed very embarrassed and replied: 'I
don't know about words...' We fell silent and soon afterwards he dropped off to sleep... Next morning, I gather, he
left, without saying goodbye or leaving word. Did I hurt his
feelings in some way?

Anyway, in order to right a possible wrong and to cement
this new and admirable extension of hands across the Irish Sea,
I have given your address to a couple of Paddies, close drinking acquaintances of mine here. Their names are Pat Cloonan
and Festy O'Donnell. Both are unmarried and in their thirties.
They are what I suppose you would call 'rough diamonds' but
none the worse for that! I'm sure Jane won't mind giving them
bed and breakfast for a while. They are only planning to spend
about ten days initially but if they like London, they may stay
on and work there. In which case, I'm sure you could come to

some arrangement for full board – something like five guin-
eas. This may seem a lot but I ought to warn you they both
have healthy appetites.

Best wishes to you all,

Tony

Of course, the two 'rough diamonds' were an invention, though Tony
– and those friends to whom he told this story – took great pleasure in
imagining my parents being too nervous to answer the door, in case Pat
and Festy turned up. But the letter should also be seen as a modest dig
at my working-class father's middle-class conventionality. My father's
answer does not survive but he would usually respond to such taunts by
mocking bourgeois Tony's romantic eccentricities.

157

At around this time, my father was working on his first mainstream
book, a Penguin anthology of modern English writing. It was an eclectic
and adventurous selection. It included prose from Naipaul and Achebe,
verse by his friends Thom Gunn, Ted Hughes and Seamus Heaney, and
lyrics by the Beatles ('Eleanor Rigby') and Pink Floyd ('Arnold Layne').
There was also the Stevie Smith poem I would read at a school assembly
and over my father's coffin. And, as my father pointed out to me, I am
referred to, implicitly, in the introduction, when my father mentions
that 'junk', as an art form, is being taught 'as a subject in infant schools'.

One day he had asked me which lesson I enjoyed most at school, and, much to his amusement, I had replied 'junk'. That led to many years of teasing.

I've been training a forensic eye on the rest of his introduction. Twice my father mocks the soap opera *Coronation Street* as a sentimentally inadequate rendering of working-class life. He must have known how much both my mother and Tony loved the programme.

And I have just noticed that he mentions Tony White at the end of the introduction, thanking him for help in making the selection. My mother and I are a bit surprised by this. She can't think why he's there in a list of only three names. It just seems a bit unlikely that he would have helped my father – Tony was one of his very few friends who never wrote for any of his magazines, and was an unlikely literary advisor. But now I think I may have worked it out, after reading Tony's letter to Thom Gunn written at about the same time, in which Tony compares the Beatles' lyrics to Auden's ballads, and singles out 'Eleanor Rigby' for special praise. And so perhaps it was Tony who convinced my father that 'Eleanor Rigby' was poetry, and deserved to be included in an anthology of modern English writing.

In the alphabetical list of contributors, John Lennon is sandwiched between Philip Larkin and Doris Lessing. I like that.

158

In 1967, Tony's father died – of a heart attack while travelling on the Underground – and my mother wrote to Tony, commiserating. She asked him if he was interested in a job at Jonathan Cape, the publishers where she was working.

Tony's response survives – a slightly subdued letter to a former lover, sent to her work address with the word 'Personal' underlined in the top left hand corner of the envelope. 'It was very nice of you to ask me [about the job]. And I expect you've found someone by now anyway. Let's meet for a chat one day. Love, Tony.'

159

My mother can't quite remember when, and her diaries give no clue, but they fleetingly became lovers again at this time, and they watched a lot of *Coronation Street* together.

160

In 1969, Tony briefly returned to the stage, in a role that has a tangential bearing on this story. He played illegitimate Edmund ('Now, gods, stand up for bastards!') in my uncle Jonathan's 1969 production of *King Lear*. He delighted his old friends and amazed his new ones with a commanding display of panache and malevolence – more than a decade after his last performance. But he hated it. And would never act again.

Instead, he continued to write and translate, and spent more and more time working as a builder. He brought together a small group of friends who worked on building projects, first in London, but then elsewhere: in Yorkshire for Ted Hughes, in the south of France for Sasha.

He sometimes referred to his informal company of builders as J.N. Limited. J.N. was short for Jesus of Nazareth, another long-haired, part-time carpenter. He signed one letter to my mother 'Tony of Nazareth'. He was better than most of us at laughing at himself.

161

Tony White was famously clumsy as a builder, for ever falling through floors and tripping over paint-pots – and he was never very interested in the business side of building. Once, in Yorkshire, he berated his open-mouthed and unpaid colleagues, accusing them of 'being only in it for the money'. This was a joke of course, but only funny because it did partially correspond with Tony's outlook on the world. He showed little interest in money, and had a tendency, very irritating to his colleagues, of charging clients too little, and of failing to collect final payments. And he did not always finish jobs.

There survives, for instance, a series of brief postcards and letters to my mother apologising for bits of unfinished work around the house in Limerston Street. Or perhaps this was an excuse for him to visit her, or even possibly to see me.

162

My first memories of Tony date from the late '60s: snapshot images of a bear-like man laughing out loud. He was the largest and loudest of my parents' friends. And my earliest clearly dateable recollection is from August 1969, when I was seven.

I have three such memories, all set in my family home – the others are from 1973 and 1975 – and they each take the form in my mind of a few seconds of film; of slightly jumpy, staccato, newsreel footage. They must have been salvaged from the recesses of my brain when I discovered that Tony was my biological father, eighteen months after his death – and they have, ever since, been played over and over again in my head.

163

The 1969 memory is part of my strongest sequence of early recollections; from the time when I was ill with osteomyelitis, and I stayed on in London with my mother while the rest of the family went on holiday to Italy. Friends of Tony's, including my future colleague Peter Doherty, were working in the house: repairing window frames, stripping the woodwork, painting the stairwell, mending the banisters.

I remember sitting on the stairs near the front door one day when Tony appeared. He called out 'Hello', in his booming voice, as he entered the already open door. His hair was wild and his trousers were torn. He smiled broadly at me. And everyone – my mother, Peter and the other builders – appeared from different parts of the house and came out to welcome him. And that, sadly, is the end of the memory.

But I do still have a sense of how his large, loud, friendly presence seemed to animate the household. Everyone was talking. They wanted Tony's attention, a piece of him.

Peter, to whom I described this scene recently, responded with his own memory from the same period. He recalled Tony sitting at the kitchen table chatting with my mother, while I sat nearby contentedly playing on a cushion on the floor, my ankle wrapped in a bandage.

Peter says he thought nothing of it at the time – but this image of the three of us remained with him forty-five years later.

164

Peter was also an actor-builder – though he was keener to continue acting than Tony. As a child, I thought of them as some kind of double act, two music-hall comedians – largely because of what became known as 'the Daffodil Dance'.

Just before my eleventh birthday, my parents had a party at Limerston Street, and I was allowed to stay up. This enabled me to witness the inaugural version of the Daffodil Dance – the second of my Tony memories, and the occasion when I learned that grown-ups could be even sillier than children, particularly after a few drinks.

The dance took place at the garden end of the living room. I sat on the desk at which my mother, by now a teacher, marked schoolbooks every evening. And I watched, with many others, as two men hit each other gently over the head with daffodils. Tony and Peter were standing opposite each other, a single daffodil in their right hands. They took it in turns to strike each other on the forehead, accompanying themselves with the most rudimentary of tunes – dip-dip-dip, I think it went – and skipping in time with the tune and the daffodil blows. Tony was broad-shouldered, long-haired and heavy-footed; Peter was a little smaller, dazzlingly handsome and far more elegant. They both took the performance very seriously. They did it once, and everyone clapped and cheered. And then more guests came into the room from downstairs and they were forced to repeat it. Everyone stopped talking in order to watch them. I remember my parents standing next to each other; my mother laughing and encouraging them to carry on. I learned the meaning of the adjective 'camp' that evening.

A week later my mother was sent a thank-you postcard by Tony and Peter, in Tony's hand-writing. The words 'Rave! Rave!' appear in the right top corner, and a heart in the top left of the card. And in the bottom left corner are two daffodils.

'Camp' was signed in Peter's handwriting, and I later discovered that 'Camp' and 'Dreadful' had become their nicknames for each other.

RAVE! RAVE!

To our favourite hostess — with thanks for enabling us to launch the entirely original "Daffodil Dance" and in anticipation of further engagements, from the two butchest flower-dancers in the business — Camp + Dreadful

The Daffodil Dance soon became their party piece. They performed it many times on the Battersea Park football tour of France later that year – including to a public audience on a cross-Channel ferry. And Tony writes to my mother again, telling her that 'the Daffodil Dance [was] a huge success on boats, but painful with plastic flowers'. Peter remembers that they drew blood.

My final memory of Tony was the one I referred to earlier, when he came to dinner and I had curdled the bouillabaisse, and he was kind to me and my family was not. My clear memory was that he came with his leg in plaster, and that this dinner happened shortly before he died. But I found another one of his postcards recently, in which he refers to the dinner, and the date is earlier than his football accident.

This troubles me because it shows that my last memory of Tony is a false one – or partially false at least. A post-mortem invention, or a conflation of what I remember and what I was told. He was as fit as a fiddle when he praised my bouillabaisse; and the full leg in plaster, and the cut-off jeans, that I seem to remember so vividly, are figments of my imagination.

But the rediscovered postcard, written from Ireland, and addressed to 'The Millers, 26 or 28 Limerston Street', also provoked in me another complex reaction, because in its text, in parentheses, he mentions me by name:

> Sorry about the vagueness of your address, but did I ever really know it. That was a fine banquet you (esp. Sammy) laid on before I left. Life is good here, weather and moods totally unpredictable. Met Seamus Heaney a few weeks back and discussed football. I'll be back in town next month for a bit, till when, love to you all,
>
> Tony

It's not easy to explain how I responded to seeing my name in Tony's handwriting – but it caused a sharp intake of breath. It was his last letter to my parents (actually it was addressed to all of us Millers) and it singled me out.

I felt pleased and sad, and it left me wondering what he might have thought of me that day. Did he consider me as his own in some way, or had he banished such ideas from his mind? And what if he had lived, and I had learned that he was my biological father? How would we have navigated our way through that, and what would we have come to mean to each other? I still struggle with answers to those questions.

166

By this time, Tony had decided that he really did not want to be in London. But after his father's death he was preoccupied by his mother, who was alone and unhappy. And for the rest of his life his concern for her restricted his choices and movement. He hoped at one point that she would move with him to Ireland, but she wouldn't, and eventually she went into a nursing home. Tony continued to 'commute' back and forth, every few weeks or months, between London and Ireland.

He was drawn more and more to the wilds of Connemara, and bought a small plot of land with a ruined cottage close to where he had lived through that first Irish winter, looking after a lobster farm. He rebuilt the cottage, and began to refer to it as home. He almost seemed ready to settle – though I do not imagine that he would have used that word. He asked at least three of his on–off girlfriends to join him in his Connemara fastness. None of them was keen, and they all doubted that he was serious about the offer. After all, as one of them pointed out to me, the cottage consisted of a single room and had no toilet. He said that he planned to live out his days there. He had, undoubtedly, a romantic vision of Ireland's western coast and its people, but he also felt that he belonged there – and the friendships he made were lifelong.

Tony's cottage stood (and still stands, modernised now, with an inside toilet), on a narrow strip of land between a lake and the sea. From his cottage, Tony could see Inishbofin, the small island where he spent many summers from the late 1950s to the mid-1970s writing, fishing, building and escaping from London. And on the island, Tony is still remembered with extraordinary warmth and unexpected detail by that small percentage of the island's population who are over sixty – and his name is known from family tales by the younger generation.

I went to Inishbofin recently, for a literary festival – incognito at first. But I was soon outed and welcomed as the natural-born son of an island hero. It is fair to say, I think, that something of a legend has grown up around Tony White on Inishbofin, and I was greeted as a less heroic look-alike. He is remembered most of all by the islanders for his willingness to lend a hand, for the way he became part of their community.

Most outsiders, or 'blow-ins' as they are known, were not able to contribute: they could not do anything useful such as dig turf, or mend a net, or sail a fishing boat. One islander said to me with great admiration, 'The thing about your father', and here he pointed out that he was quoting Seamus Heaney, was that 'he could handle a spade'.

There's something about dying young that is attractive to balladeers, and the Ballad of Tony White has taken several forms, including at least four poems by Richard Murphy. There's one poem in particular, 'Tony

White on Inishbofin', written three years after his death, which places him firmly on the island.

And at eleven o'clock one storm-ridden Saturday evening in May 2015, in front of the slightly sozzled audience of the first Inishbofin Literature Festival, which included the Irish President and the biological son of Tony White, these words were read from the festival stage.

> With lobster pot for a chair
> And a fish-box for a table
> He'd sacrificed a plausible career
> On the London stage to live near
> The sea in a bare room
> Far from home
> To become on the lips of islanders a fable.

2014:7

One evening in early September, I returned to my parents' house after a long walk through the hillocks of south London. I was amazed to see my father at his desk, tapping away at his computer keyboard. He was quite angry; the computer was, he said, 'swallowing' his words. I looked at his enormous screen; there were a few seemingly random words up there, with huge spaces in between. He was writing a book review, he told me. It was not going well. And I was secretly displeased.

Six months earlier, when he could not get down the stairs, I took over his study, and his desk. And I was now beginning to work on a book about London. My laptop had been pushed aside by my father and piled high with books and pieces of paper on which I had written my notes.

In the process several lines of gobbledegook had been entered into my own onscreen document. I tidied my things a little, holding back my irritation. After all, it was his study, his desk, and he was trying to write a review. I should have been delighted – it was unthinkable that he would have been doing this six months earlier. He looked up at me, grimly. 'I can't get the fucking computer to work.'

Earlier in the year, my father had been asked by the *Spectator* magazine to write a review of a poetry collection called *I Knew the Bride* by Hugo Williams – a friend, and someone whose work he had long admired. At the time, my father was in no condition to read anything, let alone write a book review. In August, the *Spectator* called again. Could he try once more? The literary editor, Mark Amory, was retiring, and he wanted a piece by every previous literary editor of the magazine for his valedictory issue. My father agreed, partly out of anxiety and guilt: he realised his friend's book had not been reviewed at all in the *Spectator*, because of his failure to do so earlier in the year. He had not written anything since the previous autumn.

He had attempted to read some of the poems while he was recovering, and couldn't understand them – because his mind was so tangled, and he often could not distinguish dreams from reality. But then when he was asked, again, to review the book, he took it seriously. And he and I began to read the poems out loud to each other – and discuss them. I took notes. I imagined I might write something based on what he had said about the poems to me, and I could then give that to the *Spectator* – a ghost-written book review. I began to structure, in my mind, our first ever collaboration. He looked slightly troubled when I suggested this solution. I think it may even have inspired him to get out of bed and write his own review while I went for a walk.

The review that he was trying to type up on the computer already existed, handwritten, on several scraps of paper, whose order was uncertain. The following day I typed them up, nervously, hoping that it would be a piece of writing that deserved his name on it. And to my great relief and excitement it was better than publishable. It was personal and funny, and sometimes slightly obscure, and dealt movingly with Hugo's poems about death and about hospitals. It also had a certain staccato quality which was corrected when my father read my print-out, and told me how to re-order his paragraphs.

I suggested a few minor changes, most of which he dismissed – and I emailed it to Mark Amory, one September evening, with these words, dictated to me by my father:

> I am still ill, and fear I haven't done as well with Hugo's poems as I had hoped.
>
> Please let me know if you share my sentiments.
>
> > Regards for the future,
> >
> > Karl

Mark responded early the next morning, 'Your review of Hugo's poems is elegant and touching... I am more grateful than I can remember being for any other contribution.' My father was pleased, but looked a little doubtful when I suggested he wrote some more reviews. It had been an enormous effort for him.

It was the last article he would write – and it was published, not a word altered, just four days before he died. There was, I realise now, a certain symmetry to this final piece of writing. It was a book review for the magazine at which he started his professional career in literary journalism almost sixty years earlier. The last of many hundreds of reviews he would write over that period. And it was also an understated plea for greater recognition for a poet whom he had long admired – a position he'd taken with many other poets and writers during that long career.

169

In early January 1976, Tony White was staying at the house of an Anglo-German psychiatrist in Twickenham, in south-west London. The psychiatrist was an expert on impotence, and Tony had recently taken on the task of ghost-writing his autobiography. In the late morning of Friday, 9 January, Tony called out for help from the bathroom, and then he mumbled something about his mother. He collapsed and died before the ambulance could get him to the nearest hospital. A blood clot had travelled from his leg to his lungs, and it killed him almost immediately. He was forty-five years old.

170

Less than a month earlier, Tony had been playing football for Battersea Park, when, in his own words, 'some young cowboy scythed me down as if I was an offending thistle'. Peter Doherty, who was at the other end of the pitch, heard Tony's tibia snap – a piercing crack that brought everyone on the field to a standstill. Tony was taken to hospital. His right leg was put in a heavy, full-length plaster cast, and he was sent home. Except he didn't really have a home – and he spent most of the next three weeks at the north London flat of his old school friend, John Holmstrom.

Tony kept himself busy, but was dependent on friends who would cart him around from party to pub. He was transported to the wedding of an actress friend just before Christmas, and lots of famous actors signed his cast. And that evening he went back to the flat of a long-standing girl-friend, who still lives there, with several fading photos of her long-dead lover on her dresser.

'We had it off,' she informed me, waving vaguely in the direction of the bedroom of the flat that Tony had helped her decorate more than four decades earlier. 'And then he went back to John Holmstrom's in a taxi.'

She looked up at the ceiling, as if calling the gods to account. 'He said that the plaster was uncomfortable and he didn't want to keep me up all night.' She never saw him again.

171

Then just after New Year, slightly more mobile now, Tony moved to Twickenham and returned to ghost-writing. 'The Good Doktor and his wife,' Tony wrote in his thank-you letter to John, 'are very, very kind and there is a small and affectionate dog called Parsnip who pops in now and then to see if I've got all I need.' He's still uncomfortable in his plaster, and talks about getting a new, lighter one at his next hospital appointment on Monday, 12 January. He died on Friday the 9th.

It's hard to exaggerate the grief and shock that was felt by Tony's many friends and lovers, and which some of them feel to this day, more than forty years later. The bad news was communicated by phone, around London, across the Irish Channel, to America. It was the least anticipated of deaths. Tony was strong and fit, in the best of spirits and full of plans – largely to spend more and more time in Ireland. That Friday evening in January became, for his friends, a life-marker – they would always re-member where they were when they heard of the death of Tony White.

My mother had my father to console her. And he did so; memorably for me, on that day that Tony died. It was the early evening. The phone rang, and my father answered. John Holmstrom told him what had happened. A few seconds later my father told my mother. I was downstairs, and I heard a noise, a scream I think – though I wonder if that is a figment of my over-active imagination. I remember entering the living room, and first I heard my mother's guttural sobs, and then saw the tears running down her reddening cheeks. My father, seated on the arm of the large chair next to her, was leaning in, holding her around the shoulders, so obviously concerned for her that I felt I was intruding, that I was interrupting a moment of marital intimacy.

The next few days were the hardest for my mother, since she had no one she could really talk to about her love for Tony – and she describes herself as being paralysed by grief. Though she would later tell me that my existence helped her to deal with Tony's death, that through me he might live on, vicariously.

She had, until then, told her secret to just one person – her closest friend, then living in Bristol. She decided to tell her sister, Rachel, about me and about Tony, and she remembers calming words, and the suggestion that she might go and see Tony's body before the funeral. My mother chose not to.

174

My mother can remember little in detail of the desolate days immediately after Tony's death. But one small incident has remained with her. I would turn fourteen on 13 January. And the day before my birthday, she realised she hadn't bought anything for me. She wandered, bereft and in a daze, around a London bookshop. She couldn't think what I might want. She bumped into a friend, who pointed to a two-volume boxed set of books called *How Things Work*, which would then sit on my shelves for many years.

My mother felt at the time that this was unsatisfactory as a present, and it came to symbolise some kind of guilt that she felt towards me. She was so stricken by sorrow and shock that she was unable to think about what I might want, but was clear that somehow I deserved, especially now, some grander, more significant gift. I was perfectly pleased with the book – and I would later decide, in relation to its subject, that I was far more practical than my father, but a good deal less practical than Tony.

My mother took some uncalculated risks in the frenzied days after Tony died. She went to the flat where he'd been staying before his injury, and removed a large metal box full of his belongings – mainly family papers and newspaper cuttings, as well as a small silver spoon. She isn't quite sure why, or how she got away with it. It may have been that she wished to make sure that there was nothing that Tony possessed that would reveal the truth about me – though she doesn't think this is the case. She may have been trying to save something for me that belonged to him, or she may just have wanted something of Tony's for herself.

The second risk was to take me, alone of her children, to Tony's wake. She insists this was not deliberate, and it 'just worked out like that'. I would later invest this event, the drunken, uninhibited party at Becky's Dive, with great significance, as marking the moment, in some fictional way, when I became an adult. I would also later feel foolish that I hadn't realised at this point that Tony White was my biological father. I was beginning to look like him. Richard Murphy noticed me at the wake and saw the resemblance to Tony, and wondered whether I might be his son.

My mother also befriended Tony's mother, now in a London nursing home, and visited her regularly there – making a point of seeing her on Tony's birthday, a month to the day after his death. She saw even more of Tony's old nanny, known to all his friends as, simply, 'Nanny'. No one seems to remember her real name, though her surname was Carter. And in March 1976 my mother drove Nanny to Ireland to visit Tony's cottage, and his nearby grave, where a miniature coffin with some of his ashes had been buried; a pilgrimage for both women. None of this seems to have been considered significant by others. It was as if looking after the family of the dead was women's business; that my mother was just being dutiful in helping out after the death of her husband's great friend.

177

My mother also wrote, soon after his death and for her eyes only, an incomplete novel entitled *Tales of an Adulteress*. She wouldn't show it to me for ages, but now she has – fifty-odd pages of typescript. It's a thinly disguised account of her relationship with Tony, who has been renamed Tom. I have become Simon, and the story begins with Tony's death, before describing how their relationship began in Rome.

The narrator describes how at the funeral 'Simon wandered off to inspect the wreaths, taking his strong thighs and square feet away. He had bits of Tom all right, though they were a back-handed comfort just now.'

She is anxious about how to behave at the funeral. 'Do I seem to be overdoing the grief? I am, after all, only the wife of an old friend he saw less and less often over the years… She was going to sneeze or giggle. That wasn't allowed either. A widow or mistress may giggle or weep. It is permitted. But who was she to behave in an unsuitable manner at the funeral of a man whom she'd known only at college and on football tours?'

Others felt free to grieve more publicly, and more poetically. The myth of Tony White, which he had tried to stamp out in his lifetime, soon took wing.

Sasha, for instance, who had introduced my mother to both my father and to Tony a quarter of a century earlier, and who may also have been Tony's lover, wrote a poem not long after Tony's death in which she described him as, *inter alia*, a Magus and a master of transformations.

> Did you know how passionately you were loved?
> Guru-routier, friend, master of transformations,
> Magus who linked so many disparate spirits.

While Richard Murphy, in his poem 'Tony White 1930–1976', also seemed to think that his dead friend had supernatural powers:

> His very breathing made the foul air pure
> His presence made the darkest day feel clear

John Holmstrom, in a memorial poem written soon after Tony's death, refers to him, as if he were ripe for canonisation, as 'the blessed Tony White'. While Thom Gunn's 'Talbot Road' was a little less hyperbolic about Tony, not endowing him with powers to perform miracles, but instead describing him as a mere duke:

> Friends and lovers
> All had their own versions of him.
> Fantastical duke of dark corners,
> He never needed to lie: you had learned not to ask questions

And my father would, some years later, in a prose memoir, dub Tony with the slightly more exalted title, the 'prince of panache'.

At the time of Tony's death, I discovered recently, my father, who had long since given up writing verse about anyone except his children, proposed instead a 'symposium' on Tony White. I was never able to ask what he meant by that: a memorial service of sorts, perhaps. But Thom Gunn was lukewarm about the idea, suggesting that Tony would have hated such a thing, and the symposium was stillborn.

179

For some, Tony's death was life-changing. Richard Murphy and John Holmstrom would both tell their friends that they never really recovered. One of Tony's girlfriends, Pixie Weir, is said to have been driven mad by his death – and Peter Doherty remembers finding her as she wandered the streets of Notting Hill looking for her dead lover.

She upbraided Tony's old school friend John Holmstrom for having, in an unspecified way, prevented Tony 'from leading a normal emotional life', to which John responded with vigour and sadness:

> I don't imagine any of us have been at our best since Tony's death, but most don't go around charging almost total strangers with unspecified corruptions and hypocrisies… Tony had been my dearest friend for about 30 years, so I don't imagine your loss can have been any greater than mine. I can just hear Tony (wherever he is) howling with laughter at this macabre incident – but personally I'd prefer you to feel the kind of sympathy for me that I feel for you.

In the months after Tony died, a story began to circulate among his friends that Tony had a child. And the source was Pixie. It seems that she had once teased Tony, questioning his masculinity by pointing out his childlessness. And he had risen to the bait, and told her that he did have a child, but would say no more. Many, but not all, of Tony's friends disregarded Pixie's story. She was not well, and her story of some secret love child sounded too fantastic.

My parents' lives soon returned to some sort of normality. They were in their forties, and their careers were changing direction. My father had, temporarily, no magazine to edit – and was now a full-time professor of English Literature; a journalist without a PhD parachuted into a nest of academics. My mother, too, was on her way to becoming an academic – no longer teaching in London secondary schools, but training others how to teach.

Their children, at the time of Tony's death, were eighteen, thirteen and eleven, and kept their parents busy. My older brother Daniel was a painter, like his paternal grandfather and maternal grandmother before him, and like them he knew early on what he wanted to spend his life doing. The other two of us were never so certain. My younger sister was preternaturally mature, and already a confidante to teenagers and adults. And there was me in the middle: intellectually confident, defiantly untidy and, in an innocently stubborn way, ignorant of everyone's feelings, including my own.

For almost four decades, I thought that my mother told me about Tony just a few months after he died. In my recollections of those distant teenage years, there seems to be almost no gap between his funeral and learning the truth of my paternity. But recently she let me go through her old appointment diaries, and there, inscribed in tiny blue writing, on 14 July 1977, the day after my school had broken up for the summer, she had written 'Told S'.

In fact, it was eighteen months and five days since Tony died – during which time, by my slovenly standards, I had accomplished a great deal. I had finished my O levels and played rugby for my school. I had travelled abroad without my family, to France, where I had, best of all, received, tremulously, my first kiss – from a French girl who had 'I want to sleep with you' written in English on her schoolbag.

My mother wrote her unfinished secret novel *Tales of an Adulteress* before she told me about Tony, and then put it away for almost forty years. In the novel, her character is trying to decide whether to tell Simon (me) that Tom (Tony) is his father.

> Simon came in. Barefeet and hair in his eyes, he was bigger than she was. Fourteen and mad about rugby. She'd never managed to explain properly to Tom why she wanted to tell Simon, how it interfered even with looking at him for it not to be known. He'd probably not be concentrating if she did tell him. He slipped away from advice or serious talk, padded away to his room.

184

My mother is not sure why she chose to tell me then. We were painting my bedroom, just as she and Tony had been alone together painting the kitchen of the same house sixteen years earlier, when their affair resumed, with such important consequences for me.

There are other possible explanations: Pixie's rumours about Tony's love child were doing the rounds. And I was beginning to resemble Tony more and more. She had not discussed it with my father in advance, though they had always agreed that I would have to be told one day. It was a decision taken on the spur of the moment.

My mother remembers me reacting calmly, and giving her a hug, as she cried while telling me, briefly, about Tony. My immediate reaction was to lie, and to pretend that I knew already – not about me, but that Tony had a child. I think I felt slightly humiliated by the existence of such a big secret about me, of which I knew nothing. And so I invented a story, which I told her, about having overheard her and Dad talking about Tony and his child one day. She did not question or contradict my invention.

185

Later that day, I wrote a few words in a diary – the first page in a journal that I kept sporadically for several years. It was written in code, because I knew my little sister loved nothing better than secret diaries. (She also liked to tell me that I was 'adopted' whenever I did something that she didn't think was normal.) My coding device was an English-German dictionary. I would look up each word in English, and look at the position and page number of the entry. I then moved methodically to the exact

186

place in the dictionary 200 pages further ahead and replaced the English word with the German one.

In the late nineties, when I had my own children, I found the diary – and the dictionary – and back-translated the entry. It was disappointingly winsome and uninformative. It was full of protestations that nothing had changed, and I simply swore to love my family just as much as I had before. Maybe the painstakingly slow process of coding my thoughts was a disincentive to writing up my more profound reflections, or maybe I had none.

186

There were no obvious immediate consequences. My mother told my father that I knew. But he and I did not even refer to the matter for another thirty-five years. Only one other person was told at this time: Tony's sister, Lois. She'd just met Pixie, who'd told her the story of Tony's child – a daughter, she thought. And for some reason, Lois seemed to think that my aunt Rachel was a possible mother of this unidentified child. Lois then asked my mother if Rachel had a child by Tony; and my mother was so stunned that she told her the truth. Lois told her daughters, my cousins, but no one else – and I received, at some point, the gift of Tony's old penknife. I did not hear from Tony's family for more than a quarter of a century.

Others may have guessed. Tony's nanny must have known; though my mother did not speak of it to her, and she must also have known not to ask. We'd visit her sometimes, my mother and I; we'd take her out to lunch, and she would tell my mother to give me the money to pay the bill – as if this is what teenage boys needed to learn, and that this is what she had taught Tony. We all laughed at that, because Tony was not very good with money, or never seemed to have any, and gave it away when he did. She spoke a lot of Tony, and not long before she died she gave me a silver teapot that the White family had given to her.

And I was taken to see Tony's mother a few weeks before she died; her strong French accent had been corrupted by the effects of a stroke. She may not have understood who I was, or why I was there – but surely she, of all people, even in her dotage, must have seen my now startling resemblance to her younger son.

187

Then, in 1979, I too made my pilgrimage to the place where Tony had been happiest, his Connemara cottage. It was blustery and Spartan and remote – and I picked cockles from the seashore and boiled them to make my dinner, imagining that I might not after all be such a city boy. The first cockle I tasted was inedible, like a regurgitated piece of rubber, and I took the saucepan to the front door, and threw the contents with all my strength into the wilderness. The wind was so strong that it blew the boiling water and cockles back at me, like a burning hailstorm. I realised I had a lot to learn about country ways.

I went to see Tony's as-yet-unmarked grave on Omey Island, to which he would run when the tide was low. And I took a boat out to Inishbofin, semi-incognito, as a tourist – and the shy son of a friend of Tony's – and was welcomed, as all are welcomed on that island.

Back on the Irish mainland I stayed with Tony's old friend Richard Murphy who knew, as he knew of Tony, not to ask any difficult questions.

Thirty-five years later, I travelled to another island, Sri Lanka, to visit Richard – by then in his late eighties – who had returned to live in the land of his colonial childhood. There he showed me his diaries from the seventies, and I suddenly found myself face-to-face with myself as a seventeen-year-old boy on that trip to Connemara. It was a generous but telling account.

> How strong is the resemblance of Sam Miller to Tony: he's like a reincarnation. Not just that he has the same dark hair and eyebrows, or the same brown eyes: but his impact on strangers reminds me of Tony's extraordinary attraction.
>
> On his way through Dublin at half past seven in the morning, Sam by mistake left one of his bags on a dustbin, and when he came back it was gone. He met a street-cleaner who invited him into a pub for a drink. This was near the markets where the pubs open early. The cleaner promised to keep a lookout for the bag. A couple of hours later Sam returned and met the cleaner who had found his bag in one of the dustbins. This is the kind of thing that could easily have happened to Tony on one of his fabulous excursions. Sam can effortlessly form friendships with people of any class or race, as Tony could.

Richard Murphy didn't know my father, or he would have realised that one of the many things that Tony White and Karl Miller had in common was that ability to form friendships with people of any class or race. I don't think I've been nearly as good at friendship as either of them.

We argued a lot, my father and I, during the last month of his life. The main subject of dispute was the land of his birth: Scotland (though we did also have terse words about my impending departure for my adopted country, India, as well as my failure to be more appreciative about the city of my birth: London). We fell on either side of a great debate over the future of the United Kingdom – a referendum on Scottish independence.

My father was brought up in Scotland and once spoke with a broad Scottish accent – which would return when he played football, or was angry. His best jokes were Scottish, his literary heroes – Drummond, Boswell, Burns, Hogg, Stevenson – were all Scottish, and we spent our childhood holidays in Scotland. But he would have no truck with independence: 'I was a Scottish patriot when I was young,' he wrote in his memoirs, 'but not a Scottish nationalist, and my sentiments have not changed.' The Scots, he felt – and he'd include himself – had done well out of the Union.

That last month of his felt at times like a festival of Scottishness. My father and I began working our way through the poetry and songs of Robert Burns, and read MacDiarmid and MacCaig for good measure. We joked away about MacDiarmid's line about 'Scotland's hidden poo'ers', a wonderful gift to those who love a scatological double entendre. Dad's Scottish friends appeared at Limerston Street more frequently, to discuss and debate independence with my father: Neal Ascherson said Yes, Andrew O'Hagan said No. And I vacillated for a while.

Twelve days before my father died, I went with my two children to Edinburgh to show them for the first time my childhood haunts, and those of my father. We stayed with an old friend, Alison, the older daughter of my father's oldest friend, Rob Taubman. Alison had moved back to Edinburgh a few years earlier to look after her dying parents. The visit felt like a pilgrimage.

We drove to Polwarth Rhodes, the cottage in the Borders where I had spent my childhood holidays. We went to the nearby country church in whose cemetery were buried two young men: Alison's brother, who slipped down a cliff-face in the 1970s, and the closest friend of my teenage years, who had killed himself in 1983. We visited the Royal High School in Edinburgh where our fathers had first met in the 1940s. I suggested we visit my father's birthplace, the village of Straiton – but Alison said it was now an IKEA superstore – and I felt no desire to go there.

But we did go to 54 Moredun Park Gardens, the bungalow in Gilmerton on the outskirts of Edinburgh, which I remembered so happily from my childhood, and where my father had lived from the age of two. Gilmerton had been gentrified, and the coal mine was long gone. There was a shiny silver-coloured car parked in what was once the front yard of the bungalow, while a wooden deck had been constructed in the back garden. We were invited in by the woman who had bought the house from my great-aunt's estate, and had raised her family there. She showed us the title deeds and there was Margaret Connor's name writ large, though she was always Peggy to me. The house, though, seemed even smaller – and we all wondered how, in my father's time, so many of them, five normally, sometimes six, could have lived in such a tiny space.

I took photos of my children posing outside his old home, and emailed them from my phone to my mother in London – who then showed them on her laptop to my father. 'Don't tell him where I am. See if he recognises it.' He did, after a while – fooled briefly by the unexpected sight of a car in front of the freshly painted house, with its new red trimmings. I wanted him to feel as if he might be there, a vicarious visit to his ancestral home. And when I went back to London I showed him all the photos, and many memories came tumbling out.

But by the time I returned I had become, to my father's irritation, something of a Scottish nationalist. I'd been turned, and told my father that if I had a vote, I'd vote Yes for independence. 'It's lucky you don't,' he said, but then he didn't have one either. He accused me of romanticising Scotland – and in one long tirade against romantic nationalism referred to Robert the Bruce, Lord Byron, Gabriele D'Annunzio, and Tony White's Hibernophilia. The truth is that I was more of a contrarian than a romantic – and there was something enjoyably ludicrous about a very English son arguing in favour of independence with his Scottish father. I liked getting a rise out of my father. We kept teasing each other to the very end.

The Friday before he died, we went out to lunch – my parents, my brother, my daughter and me – ostensibly to celebrate my daughter's departure for university. But overnight the referendum had been won by the No vote, and my father was happy over his sea bass, and generously triumphant – though it had been a close-run thing.

That lunchtime I took a series of photos of him, sitting next to my daughter in Carluccio's restaurant. He'd not looked as happy all year. Still pale and thin, something of his old energy and interest in life had returned.

And he was organising a dinner for the Sunday, and telling me off for my plans to go to India on Monday evening. His dinner took place, and was a triumph – though he seems to have forgotten to invite one

of his friends, and there was a lot of shouting down the phone at the missing guest.

The following day I went to India, where I would stay for three weeks, to meet an old girlfriend and take part in a literary festival. He was resting when I left, and I kissed both his cheeks as he lay on his bed, and he blew a kiss back at me, pouting his lips. The next time I saw my father he was in his coffin.

188

I grew up, and moved into adulthood with my own fables of Tony White. I romanticised myself both as a love child, and the bearer, in my very person, in my genes, of a great secret. But in those days it never felt like my secret; it was my mother's, really, and to a lesser degree my father's.

Logically, and I once placed great store by logic, it was of no importance whose sperm helped create me. And I cannot pretend that, in my teens and early twenties, my paternity took up a great part of my thoughts. I spoke to no one of Tony, and would simply listen when others spoke of him, conscious that I should not betray too great an interest.

It was different with my mother, of course, who wished to tell me about Tony, and with whom there was no dissimulation. But I asked her almost nothing in those days.

189

Many people I knew did talk of Tony; family friends mainly, but also fellow builders and footballers. They did not know that I was his son, though some of them now say they had their suspicions. In order to earn money while I was at school and at university, I worked on small building sites for £12 pounds a day. I was large and strong, and would work hard, and loved knocking down walls. My employer, Tom Paine, and my colleague, Peter Doherty (of Daffodil Dance fame) were family friends – and it was natural that, like my brother before me, I would work with them. But they were also recent friends and colleagues of Tony's – and they too would tell tales about this man who had so suddenly disappeared from their life.

They were less reverential than the poets about Tony. They adored him, but knew his limitations – how he blundered about building sites, his inability to deal with money, to complete his latest writing or building project, or to decide what he would do next.

'He was clumsy and fearless,' Peter told me recently, 'at football and on building sites. He wasn't a skilful player, but he never stopped running. And he liked to make things more difficult for himself. He would delib- erately paint a huge wall with a tiny brush – and one time when he went to lunch, I painted the whole thing with a roller, and he couldn't believe it when he came back. He was so annoyed with me.'

Peter was also a regular player for Battersea Park, the team set up by my father and Tony – and I joined too, for a season, as an attacking left half with a dodgy knee and more energy than skill. I scored one in-glorious goal: deflected in, unknowingly, off the back of my head. Peter would tell me later that I had even less skill as a footballer than Tony.

190

The other person who talked of Tony a great deal was my father. And this is more complex territory. He spoke about Tony warmly, teasingly, as if there were no complications to the story, and to his relationship with his old friend. It was as if he didn't know I was Tony's son. Of course, he did – and, one day, late in his life, we would talk about it all. But in the late 1970s and '80s, I would find myself catching my breath when he spoke of Tony – as if some spark of jealousy or mistrust might appear. And there was none. Not a sign of it. He loved his old friend, and it was as if he had buried the information about my paternity and my mother's affairs with Tony in a completely different part of his brain.

191

According to my mother, my father never felt jealous – or at least never showed it. He did feel guilt, however (and admitted this to me later in his life), and it's possible that subconsciously at least my mother's relation-ship with Tony made him feel less guilty about his other relationships.

At one point, it seemed possible that my father might unknowingly have had a son, of about my age, with another woman, and that, even more bizarrely, this putative son – as a young man – had become a friend of my sister. It all proved untrue, but one result of the confusion and uncertainty was that my siblings, in the early 1980s, were told about Tony White.

192

I never felt that my father treated me differently from my siblings. And most of the time it would never have even occurred to me that he might. One of the reasons I have been so unwilling to tell others the story of my paternity is because on the few occasions when I have (usually to a girlfriend), the most common response has been a paean of praise about how wonderfully generous my father had been, to my mother and to me. And this has made me a little uncomfortable. Because I just don't believe he thought about it like that. Being my father was, I think, effortless for Karl Miller.

My sister recently described one telling incident that took place not long after she learned about me and Tony. She said that my father and I had quarrelled, as we did fairly often, and we were not speaking to each other. She tried to intervene, ticking my father off, and suggested to him that I might think he was treating me differently because I was not his. He just said to her, 'That's nonsense'.

This is not to say that he did not think about all these issues. In his memoirs, he writes of how, when his grandmother and aunts took him in, 'they looked after me without making a performance of it, as if it were a natural thing.' I think it felt quite natural for him to look after me; and though I am even less of an orphan than he was, he may even have seen me as some sort of kindred spirit.

193

As young adults, we were alike intellectually – we had the same bookish confidence in our own powers of communication, a belief that anything could be understood if it were well-written. And we both had a desire, more gentle in him, to cut through the verbiage of academia, and other professional languages. We both saw ourselves as journalists, and he helped me take my first few steps in that profession. But I also had a desire to wander, which he did not have – and which he never tired of objecting to in me.

194

In 1984, I went to Syria to learn Arabic, and on my return was published for the first time – in a magazine dealing with Middle East politics. It was an article about the Christians of Damascus, even then imperilled. The editor pointed out that I would not be able to return to Syria if I used my real identity. So I chose 'Robert Darke' as my alias, borrowing my father's pseudonymous surname, and prefixing it with my own middle name.

As an epigraph for his second book, *Doubles*, for which I compiled the index, my father inserted a poem, called 'Family Life', by a certain James Darke. Its subject, announced in its opening lines, is maternal abandonment:

> I thought I saw my mother. There were snaps
> Of someone else's children in her hand...

And at the end of the poem he tracks down his mother, the 'mother of my dreams', in some 'dingy place' where he found her:

> Flat out in bed. And yet it was as if
> I had to break the door down to get in.

James Darke, the poet, did not exist. He was, of course, my father – and he was also, appropriately for the book, my father's double. This was a kind of joke, a Karlian paradox, but also a way for my father to insert himself, at the very outset, into the most professorial of his writings – as well as talk about the pain of abandonment and orphanhood.

Doubles is a whirlwind of a book, ripping its way through the canon of English literature from Shakespeare to Martin Amis via Milton, Keats, Sylvia Plath and John Lennon. It is a fiercely opinionated investigation of duality in literature, and, as always in my father's writings, the personal and the literary are hopelessly and happily entangled.

He begins *Doubles*, after his pseudonymous epigraph, with a story about his aunt Peggy in her dying days. He describes how she would run away from her nursing home, and usually trip and fall over. My father recalls one of their last conversations.

> Karl: If you keep running away, you'll fall on your nose again.
> Peggy: I recognise it. But I'll do it. I'll be running away for the rest of my life. I'm two people rolled up into one.

And so flight and multiple personality, introduced here by his ageing aunt, emerge as threads that run through this book (and my father's other writings). Many of the great characters in literature, and some of their creators, are themselves two, or more, people rolled up into one, and they are usually fleeing from something or someone, often themselves.

My father's emphasis is on duality and multiple personality within one person, 'two souls which may share a breast' – but occasionally he steps into a world of more distinct doubles; of twins and doppelgangers. He writes at length of John Lennon's killer, who sometimes behaved as if he were Lennon himself; and then concludes with the briefest of stories – well-remembered in Limerston Street – of the disturbed former university student who began calling himself Karl Miller. This particular double would send my father cryptically menacing notes, of a literary kind, and telephoned my father claiming that he was watching our front door. We changed our phone number and he disappeared from our lives. He was just one of my father's many putative doubles, including the long-dead Scottish writers, William Drummond, James Boswell and Hugh Miller.

Karl Miller never wrote about Tony White as if he were his alter ego, but there is an interesting theory along these lines to be developed about their lives, which I think would have intrigued my father.

The two of them began as opposites: a well-off, London boy in a nuclear family, and a poor Scottish boy deserted by his parents. Their lives converged in post-war Cambridge, and they built an immediate friendship, and over the years they had many 'interests', including my mother and poetry and football, in common. And they chose, quite carefully and deliberately, in a way that letters (in Tony's case) and memoirs (my father's) reveal, the lives they wanted – very different lives from each other.

And so they end up again as opposites, having crossed somewhere in the middle, their worlds reversed: an impecunious, homeless, unmarried, childless jack of all trades – and a successful editor and academic with a house in Chelsea, and a wife and three children. And through all this they remained strangely dear to each other, as if they saw each other in themselves.

These felt like real choices, amidst a sea of alternatives. Such choices were not possible in the war years, or during the immediate post-war Britain of National Service and rationing. But by the mid-1950s, especially if you were young, male and confident almost everything seemed possible – even class and accent did not hold back my father, as they would have thirty years earlier.

My mother's time, and that of many women of her generation, would come later. She rarely felt she had the power to make a choice, and drifted into adulthood, and a world of work and babies. Her first real decision was me. And, after floating in and out of publishing, she made the decision to become a school teacher, a teacher of teachers – and, eventually, like my father, a professor, a writer, an editor and a journalist.

198

In her secret novel, my mother describes how her husband, renamed Henry, 'wanted a marriage and children and rooms and chairs, an address. Tom had been born with possessions and needed to lose them. Henry had nothing and needed them now.'

199

By the mid-1980s, I too was faced with decisions about what to do with my life. In distant retrospect it feels as if I was choosing between two alternatives: to be like Tony or to be like Karl, though I certainly didn't articulate this to myself in such a binary fashion. For a while, I toyed with continuing to work on building sites, earning enough money to travel and perhaps teach English or do a bit of journalism in places that were as far away from London as possible.

But then I chose my father's path, with little obvious effort or questioning. I found myself in a good steady job at the BBC. I got married and commuted to work on the Central Line. I became a householder. And for me bringing up children would seem like the most natural, most pleasing of things; half a life's work, I like to think, especially now that my children are grown.

But in all of this I remained, particularly in the world of work, as friends and colleagues would point out, a serial resigner, and a contrarian. I never felt comfortable as part of the ruling class at the BBC, and did not always know how to hold my tongue. I left and re-joined the organisation several times (it still, slightly to my surprise, employs me occasionally). These contrarian tendencies can also be seen as my father's traits – in fact his departures, from a succession of magazines, were more dramatic and irreversible than mine. Neither he nor I was scared of unemployment. We weren't in search of wealth, and each had a confidence that we would be employable and even if we weren't we would have plenty to keep us busy and interested – and that we wouldn't starve. And I was able to travel and live and work elsewhere – in Belfast, first, and then India, Sri Lanka, Tanzania and Nigeria. In that I was most unlike my father.

Tony White was not entirely forgotten. But after I told my wife-to-be about him in 1986, I revealed the secret to no one else for more than twenty years. I had a tendency to avoid self-analysis, which sometimes irritated my loved ones, and I would make a joke out of my desire not to 'dwell on the past' in spite of, and in sharp contrast to, my love of history.

My mother would sometimes want to talk about Tony, and so we did. I fear I was often a bit of a prig – and once told her that I wouldn't want the kind of complex love lives that the three of them – Karl, Jane and Tony

– led for much of their adulthood. And I had decided that I would be faithful to the person I married, according to my mother, who reminded me of this conversation recently.

My father, meanwhile, would continue to tell stories about Tony, as if the only connection was that he had been a great friend of the family, and someone whom he missed greatly. With others, I avoided the subject of my paternity, even when pressed by those, such as my wife, who knew the whole story. It felt as if there was nothing that I, or anyone else, could learn about myself from the life of Tony White; and that the circumstances of my conception were an ancient irrelevance.

202

But, in all honesty, I did have occasional instants of unnerving self-consciousness, of momentary disequilibrium, when anyone spoke of illegitimacy and bastards – even while watching a football match. Even though I wasn't sure if I was, technically speaking, a bastard, just as my father wasn't technically an orphan.

I first encountered Edmund's 'gods, stand up for bastards' speech in a student production of *King Lear*, and began to note the various literary versions of the bastard. Edmund was bad, on the whole; Esther in *Bleak House* was almost perfect; and Cosette in *Les Misérables* was too good to be true; Smerdyakov in *The Brothers Karamazov* was quite appalling – strangling cats as a child, and, as an adult, killing his father. Female bastards have had a better deal than their male counterparts.

I wondered, for instance, if people might refrain from using the word bastard in front of me if they knew my story. And did my family deliberately avoid the word? I don't know – maybe it wasn't a natural part of their vocabulary. And they may not have even associated me with the word. Maybe I am more of a cuckoo in the nest, than a bastard.

I came across no likeness, no one in literature or in life, who seemed similar to me, who was brought up as the middle child of a married couple, and then learned his father was not really his father, and that the two men were friends and remained friends. I have not yet met my double. And my situation, my story, seemed both unusual and, in the way it all played out, surprisingly uncomplicated.

203

It could have been quite different. Obviously so, if my father had responded differently to the news of the cuckoo in his nest.

But I have also often wondered – and still do – what my life, and those of others, would have been like if Tony had lived. His early death sometimes seems like an unlikely plot device, a means of tidying up the story. Would I have been told about Tony? And when? My mother says it was always her intention to tell me at some point, and she says that this was understood by my father and Tony. Given that I was beginning to look more and more like Tony, it seems hard to suppose that I wouldn't have suspected the truth. But I have learned that many of us are fallible about such things, and that we tend to believe what we want to believe.

And then I try to imagine that first meeting between me and my 'natural' father, after I had learned the truth. Would we have wanted to meet, alone, somewhere? Perhaps I would have travelled to Ireland to see him. And how would we have been with each other? Would we have hugged, or been a little stiff, or coy, or embarrassed with each other? I think probably the last. Would we have wanted to know each other better, spend time together? And how would my father have felt about that? Would I have felt pulled in two directions; would I have been worried that my father would see me as some kind of traitor?

The fact that I will never know the answers does not stop me speculating. And it's possible, of course, that nothing much would have changed. We might have acknowledged the facts, known that we all knew, and no more – and got on with our lives. All the men in this story have shown themselves quite able to hide secrets, as if they could be consigned to a different part of one's brain, squirrelled away for an emergency or for a deathbed speech, and then to behave – almost – as if they had never known the secret. But, and this is important, we also each had our sentimental side.

204

Outwardly, Tony bristled at sentimentality – but I have discovered, or perhaps invented, another more sentimental aspect to him – with the help of some old photographs. Not long ago, my mother found a brown envelope at the back of her cupboard, labelled 'Tony', in which she kept some secret things: photos, letters and postcards, a train ticket from that Italian holiday, a cork from a long-forgotten bottle of wine – shared, she imagines, with Tony. Among these items was that photo of her and Tony in Sicily which had been folded, accidentally I presume, in such a way that my mother's eyes and the top half of her face were missing. It was a lovely photo, beautifully composed, ruined by effacement. I even thought of scanning it, and attempting to use Photoshop to restore her eyes and the rest of her face.

And then, just a few months later, Richard Murphy's daughter gave me a few photos which her father had lifted from the Connemara cottage not long after his friend died. Most of them were from the 1970s and showed Tony's cottage in different states of construction, and could only be of interest to amateur builders. But, among them, miraculously, there was a copy of the same Sicilian photo and this time both faces were clearly visible. My mother and I were amazed to see this, and she was particularly pleased and surprised to discover that this man who boasted of his lack of possessions, who wanted no attachments, had kept this photo for so long and with such care.

205

Then there is a second, more complex, photo mystery. Inside the brown envelope from my mother's cupboard was another, smaller unmarked packet of photographs. I emptied the packet onto my father's desk, and out tumbled a series of images of me, Sam Miller, from the age of almost nothing to a wavy-haired teenager. There were eighteen of them. Their provenance is not clear, and my mother's memory is hazy on the subject – though only she can have been the original source of them.

I do not know for sure whether these photos were ever actually in Tony White's possession – but I like to think that they were. My mother says it's possible she took them from his London lodgings after his death. But, if so, it's not clear whether she had just given them to him when they met for what turned out to be their final evening together, a couple of months before he died. Or did she, as I suppose I hope, give them to him one by one, and did he keep them all as a little collection that grew, like me, over the years? And of course I wonder what he felt as he looked at those photos. And again I have to be content with uncertainty, and accept that I will never know.

An old friend of Tony's sent me yet another photograph recently which made me a little sad and thoughtful. It shows Tony, wild of hair, in a jeans jacket, sitting at a table next to a young girl. It's the early 1970s, and the girl is about ten – roughly my age at the time. If one didn't know better one would think them father and daughter. They are both serious, relaxed but concentrating hard; entirely unaware of the photographer. And there is a melancholy, tender air to Tony. The girl is thinking, a pencil in her hand, one end pressed to her lips. She is drawing or writing something that we cannot see. But Tony can see it, and he too is deep in thought, as if advising her on what to write next, but also as if he is pondering other matters.

And here my imagination takes flight. I have decided that in this photo Tony is wondering what it would be like to be a father, my father. And thinking that he may have missed out. Because, and I speak largely as a father here, it may have been more his loss than mine. I have two children. Tony had no children, or none that he knew.

One of the memorable things about the day my father fell down the stairs was how nice he was about each of us. He was anyway affectionate towards his family in a way that most men of his generation were not. He was tender and demonstrative, and liked to pull our earlobes and our cheeks – sometimes painfully – as a sign of love. But on 24 September 2014 it was as if he made a special effort to say something particularly pleasing or funny about each of us. He praised my brother and my sister to my mother, and, after he did so, he cupped her cheeks. And I had 'Rufty McTufty' sung down the phone to me four thousand miles away. I liked that, it warmed me, and it warms me still. But it also got me thinking.

Over the years, my father talked and wrote a great deal about suicide. He described his suicidal thoughts in his teenage journal. And there was that meticulous consideration, in his memoirs, of the circumstances of the death of his father, William, in a south London bedsit. He decided, on balance, that William had deliberately gassed himself. Part of the evidence that he weighed so carefully was that William had previously taken a knife with him on a hospital visit – to stab himself in case 'the news was bad'.

And the final chapter of my father's memoirs has suicide as its binding theme. The chapter begins by looking at the unhappy death of someone he refers to as his 'namesake' and 'alter ego', the nineteenth-century Scottish poet, memoirist, editor and geologist Hugh Miller. This unrelated Miller was in such pain, from a variety of ailments, that he put a bullet through his heart. My father then sets out a series of complex coincidences that seem to connect Hugh Miller's life (and death) to his own and that of William Miller. He and I argued once about coincidences – by which my father set great store. When I suggested that coincidences were just a lot more likely than most people realised, I remember him looking at me with annoyance, as if I'd just punctured his balloon. I have come to be more respectful of coincidences.

On the third-to-last page of his memoirs, my father declares that 'suicide and superstition are features of this book which I did not anticipate when I began to write it'. He is surprised, as I was on re-reading it, to see how much there was about killing oneself. And he continues, in those final pages, reaching an apogee of suicidal references at the end of the book. On the penultimate page, he announces, apropos of nothing in particular, and twenty-one years before he died, 'I have no plan to commit suicide', as if it were something he had been considering, but had now ruled out.

And the final sequence, on the last page of his memoirs, begins with another of my father's poems – about a man who retires from work early:

> 'For my retirement
> Present,' his wife
> Was told, 'I fancy
> A silver knife.'
> 'Salvers are safer,'
> Replied his wife,
> 'And much less handy
> For ending life.'

He wrote that poem on the day before his birthday, his sixty-first, and, in the last paragraph of the book he recalls how, the next day, he was given a silver paper-knife as a present by my mother. 'It has,' he concludes, 'a blade less sharp than the one my father took with him to hospital.'

There is another strange aspect to all this. More coincidences, per-haps. My father was no stranger to falling down stairs, literally and in verse. On one occasion, in the seventies, he was heading to my broth-er's room, ready to tell him off for not doing his homework. He tripped on the stairs, and broke his outstretched index finger on my brother's bedroom door. The admonitory finger was in a splint for weeks. And then my father and sister were co-authors, many decades ago, of an odd piece of dream-doggerel, whose prescient words now seem rather shocking.

I saw my Daddy fall down the stairs
Trinka, trinka, Jane was there.

And on that final day, my mother was alone with my father in the house. After lunch she offered to help him back up the stairs, as one of us usually did. He turned down that offer, and said he was fine, and could manage on his own. A minute or so later he fell.

None of this proves anything. I am perhaps guilty of being drawn in by the kind of coincidences my father loved so much. The rest of the family do not think that he killed himself. Rather, that he slipped, or lost balance, or had a heart attack on the stairs. I change my mind, from day to day. I know he wanted to die, but that is quite different from killing oneself.

Yet I am still left remembering the times he tentatively raised the subject of suicide in his final months, and how inadequately I responded; frozen by his words, pretending he hadn't really meant them, uttering some piffling platitude. And so I continue to wonder. Did he wait for a moment when his children were all out of the house? And did he choose to fall? I will never know for sure.

In 2004, when I was living in Delhi, I received an email sent by someone called Sue Preston from a company with the name Trillium. I didn't read it. Trillium was the name of a company to which the BBC had recently outsourced the management of its buildings – and I was about to leave the BBC. It seemed like a safe email to ignore, and I deleted it. A few weeks later, I received a second email from the same person – with the subject line: 'Cousins'. I opened it this time. I discovered that the Trillium which Sue Preston worked for was a different company. And that her reasons for getting in touch with me had nothing to do with the BBC.

Sue explained that she was the daughter of Tony White's sister, Lois. She wanted to know whether I had seen her previous email, and asked whether I wished to be in touch. I said 'No', and 'Yes', to her two questions. She then re-sent her original mail. It was a letter that touched me.

Sue wrote that she had few relatives left – her younger sister and her father had died some time ago, and her mother had just had a stroke. There were no children, no other siblings, and no cousins – except for me. 'I hope you don't mind me writing like this to you. I think my mother's recent illness has made me acutely aware of just how small my family has become. Trying to contact you was just possibly a way of making it a little bigger.'

She wrote at length about Tony, describing how she and her sister, growing up in Norwich, had idolised him, 'because he represented the antithesis of our dreary provincial childhood world. He was different, bohemian, unconventional, exciting and our favourite relative.' I liked this account of him. And I rather liked the idea that my own nieces might think of me in the same way.

I did have one moment of discomfort, though, on reading Sue's letter. She referred to Tony White as 'your father', the first time anyone had ever done so. And that made me uneasy – as if I was being encouraged to take a position, to decide on my loyalties. And there was no doubt in my filial mind, then and now: Karl Miller was, is, and always will be my father. Tony White was a half-forgotten secret.

208

I had barely thought about Tony in those early years of the new millennium, when work and children seemed to dominate my life – though on reflection I can see the small ways in which I was becoming a little more like him. In his early forties, he decided to break with London and move abroad. I had done the same – albeit with a family in tow. I had decided I didn't want a nine-to-five job, for which I might be expected to wear a tie and agree with my boss. I had become less strait-laced, less priggish, less judgemental, for instance, about matters of fidelity. I did not feel I had anything to prove to my peers. I was less anxious. I did not feel the need for certainty in my life as I once had. Conventionality seemed to have lost its appeal.

All this may just have been my version of a midlife crisis, but it felt like more of an awakening. I credited my young children, ten and nine in 2004, with this change. I wanted to spend more time with them, and less with my colleagues. And so I chose to leave full-time employment, and work from home. We'd already been moved to India – my wife's country – and we stayed on.

On my next visit to Britain I met Sue and went up to Norwich to visit Lois. She was struggling to recover from the stroke that had prompted her daughter to write to me, and she was just about to move from her home of fifty years into sheltered accommodation. Lois was eighty by then, and was very keen to talk about her two dead brothers – and was delighted when I started taking notes. Her older brother, Alan, had been killed during the war, at the Battle of Monte Cassino – he was a poet and an artist; Tony was the youngest of the three.

Lois was self-consciously conventional and would, repeatedly, compare herself unfavourably with her brothers. She described herself as the opposite of Tony – unadventurous and unimaginative. For her, having a French mother was the great embarrassment of her childhood. It made her stand out, and she wanted to fit in, and be 'ordinary'.

She was five years older that Tony and as a teenager was often tasked with his care. She recalled, guiltily, as if I were her confessor, that she would sometimes hit Tony and make him cry for no reason. She described him as being a 'very normal' child, who was rather spindly, and fell ill all the time.

'He changed later,' she said, 'I don't know why.' It might have been because of National Service, she explained, or a kind of delayed reaction to Alan's death – but he suddenly seemed quite different, full of ideas and adventures and strange notions. 'He was one of the first of the hippies,' she said, a phrase she would repeat every time she talked about him. 'My husband and Tony were complete opposites. Mike was a maths teacher. He wanted everything just so. His meal on the table at the same time each day.' She described how Tony turned up one day at her parents-in-law's house and he was unshaven and in very dirty clothes. Her husband was furious and there was some kind of scene. 'After that, I didn't see so much of Tony. But the girls just adored him.'

I visited Lois once a year, in Norwich, until her death in 2013, and she would tell me many tales of Tony's childhood and youth, and their occasional later meetings. She admitted that she didn't understand him, but as the years passed she came to admire him for his unconventionality. She had told a few of her friends about me and my secret, and she told me, with some surprise, that 'they weren't shocked' – as if this granted her permission to treat me fully as her nephew. I realised that seeing me was an important event of her year, and by the end she had even begun to confuse me with Tony.

210

I also became friends with Sue, 'my secret cousin', and gradually over this period Tony White began to grow in my mind, filling out in my wandering imagination, and becoming almost tangible. I could picture him – as did Sue and Lois – in me. His relatives had begun to draw me gently into Tony's world.

And so I found myself beginning to make comparisons with Tony, searching for coincidences and genetic predispositions. In my forties, I looked eerily like him – ungreyed with a mop of dark hair, a face dominated by a broken nose and yellowing, uneven teeth; and the shoulders, chest and legs of a bodybuilder. Lois always repeated that the top half of my head was identical to Tony's – 'You're like twins'. And I became obsessed with running – as he had been towards the end of his life.

When I turned forty-five, in 2007, I noted to myself that this was the age at which Tony died – as if I needed to be especially careful for the next twelve months. I was writing a lot: travel articles and book reviews, and then my first book – about Delhi – was published in 2009. It was a personal book in many ways. I had come a long way from the teenager who would sooner take a vow of silence than express my feelings. And there I described how living in India had brought me a new kind of freedom. 'I am no longer one of the crowd. I no longer feel the need to conform, or to measure myself against my London contemporaries. Here it is taken for granted that I am different, eccentric. I stick out wherever I go.' I think Tony White may have felt the same in Connemara.

My father was aware of my new-found relatives, and that involved the tacit acknowledgement of the Tony White connection. I would tell him I was off to see Tony's sister in Norwich – and he would sigh at the thought of such a long journey. But we said no more.

In 2010, my brother let slip to his daughter the ancient family secret – that I was someone else's biological son – and a cryptic Facebook message appeared: a message of amazement from one of my nieces to another. It was time to tell my own children, now older than I was when my mother told me. We sat on a double bed in Delhi, and I explained to them why I didn't look like my siblings. It was all a long time ago, I said, stating the obvious. They were briefly amazed, and then returned to their mobile phones and laptops. I did feel I had been able to rebalance their image of the older generation; their grandparents, in particular, suddenly seemed a little racier, and more open-minded than many of their own contemporaries.

That summer, I took my children to meet Lois, now frail and birdlike and in a residential home. My son reminded her of a teenage Tony, in a way that brought tears to her eyes. Zubin, six foot tall, bent down and gave her a hug which I thought might squeeze the life out of her. Roxy pushed her around in a wheelchair, and had a ride in it herself.

213

It was not until 2011 that I spoke to my father about it all. I had often thought about broaching the subject with him, but I did not know how to do so, and had a slightly irrational fear of the consequences. As my father grew older and weaker, I vacillated. Did I need to speak to him about Tony before he died, or was this just some selfishness on my part? Why do something that might upset us both? We got on so well in those days, though we lived in different continents. In some ways, despite the intercontinental separation, I had become even more dependent on him. He would read and edit every word I wrote. I would spend a month or so each year in the family home, and we would discuss everything – including my marriage, which had just broken up – everything except my paternity.

In the summer of 2011 I had a new project in mind: to write about the unreliability of memory. I wished to take six important incidents from my childhood and youth, and write down my account of them. And once I had done that I would seek out others who remembered that incident – an old teacher who got me expelled from my primary school, or my first lover, for their versions. I imagined there would be significant and interesting differences. I began at home, with the first two incidents – when I was very ill as a seven-year-old child, with osteomyelitis, and the events leading up to my expulsion from Bousfield Primary School at the age of eight. And my first interviewee was my father.

And so, one August day, not long after my father's eightieth birthday, I sat at his bedside, notebook in hand, taking down his account of my childhood illness and my expulsion from school. Indeed, I was right, there were some significant and interesting differences – although, I later decided, just before I dropped the project, that they were only significant or interesting to me. The interviews over, my father asked me what other incidents I wanted to look at. I told him: the suicide of my closest childhood friend, the first time I had sex, and some foolish escapade at university. 'That's five,' he said, 'not six.' And then, nervously, as if I wasn't sure if I was being prompted, I said the words, '…and Tony White.'

It was all rather elegant, on reflection – the manner in which we had segued into the subject. Neither of us had planned this – though we both soon admitted that there was a sense of relief to be talking about Tony, even if we were really talking about ourselves. It was a sentimental conversation. We both found slightly embarrassed ways of saying how much we loved each other, and that the genetic or physical facts of my paternity had made no difference. It felt as if my father was leading the discussion, as if he had prepared for it over the years, and I hadn't.

He explained that he had been anxious, after Tony's death, when my mother told me about the secret. 'I thought you handled it well,' he said. 'I was braced for trouble, but I was very moved that you treated me as your father.' He worried that it might all have burdened me, and said so in a way that implied it had not burdened him. 'It hasn't,' I replied. I took his hand, and kissed his cheek, and thanked him. And that was it. There wasn't much more that we needed to say. I could, looking back, have asked him much more, about how he felt about Tony and my mum – whether he was jealous or upset by their relationship – but the discussion was about me and him.

He then talked about his own childhood – about not having a father, about poverty, about how he didn't have proper underclothes and how shameful that seemed to him as a child. His self-esteem was low, then, and he felt he was discriminated against for being working class. He was amazed, he said, how confident I was as a child. He then did talk more about Tony, footballing stories mainly, and it was suddenly as if he had forgotten the conversation we had just had, and he had reburied the information about Tony being my biological father into the corner of his brain from which it had just been disinterred.

215

I don't think the conversation fundamentally changed our relationship, though I was pleased and relieved that it had happened. My father had two cancers by then – and in 2012 fell very ill. I thought he was about to die, though we discovered later that his strange mixture of mania and near-paralysis was almost certainly the result of a serious urinary infection. I decided I would spend more time with him. I realised that I would find it hard to forgive myself if he died while I was away.

Looking back, this may have been as much about me as him, a fear of parental mortality, perhaps a reminder of my own. But that's not how it felt at the time. I just wanted to spend more time with him; and for my children, now almost adults, to know him better. We didn't exactly move back to London, but my children were finishing school and en route to British universities. And I stopped working in India, and became something of a nomad, taking up short-term jobs in Tanzania and Nigeria, and gave myself the freedom to spend more time in the house in which I was born, in the company of those who nurtured me.

As it turned out, I was not there when my father died, and I regret that. But I have come to think that he may have wanted it that way.

EPILOGUE

I had never stood alone before an open coffin until that October morning. Inside the coffin was my father, or a resemblance of my father, his double perhaps. I leaned forward to touch the skin of his unshaven cheek, as if to see if it was really him, and then something in me pulled back my hand. I did not want to remember his skin as cold; I wanted to remember it as it was when I last touched him, when I kissed his warm cheeks in his overheated bedroom thirteen days earlier, before I left for India. But I also realised that in most ways this wasn't really him.

I had practised my speech in my head. But I couldn't begin. I knew he couldn't hear me, for – sadly – I do not believe in heavenly things. When people I love have died I always wish that I did believe in God and the transmigration of souls and all of that, because I think it would be a great comfort to believe in some kind of continuity between life and death. But still I stood over my father's body, and tried to force myself to imagine that I might join him somewhere one day, and we could compare notes on life and death, tell jokes, read poetry and even have a little kick-about. Karl Miller and Tony White as captains, perhaps, and I would join Karl Miller's team, but I might half-accidentally lose the ball to Tony, and he would score a great goal, and we would all be happy. But it's nonsense really; I know that heaven et al. are ideas that are fed to us to provide comfort, and perhaps to stop us going mad with grief. And here I was in front of my father's coffin and perhaps I was going a little mad. I broke down, and burst into sobs.

And then I steeled myself as I always know I can do at times of crisis. There is something solid, rooted deep within me that stops me ever going mad, or falling apart, or becoming depressed. I am as sturdy as an oak when I need to be, for myself, or my mother or my children. Sturdy and sentimental at the same time, that's me. And so I pressed on with my peroration, standing upright before my father's coffin, before my father's corpse, small hiccoughs of grief interrupting my flow.

'Dad,' I began, and fell silent, as if there was still some infinitesimally small chance of a response. 'Dad, do you remember how you always said, every time I went away, that the next time I would see you, you would be in your coffin? And here you are, and you were right, and I am sad and sorry. I should have stayed, that was foolish of me – I regret that more than words can say. But I know, as well, that you wanted to die, and that you may not have wanted me to see you die. Still I regret that I was not there.

'You were a father and more to me. My life might have been so different if you had been a lesser man. So I do feel some kind of special gratitude towards you, though I also feel the word gratitude is somehow misplaced here. Because it was part of your very being to treat me as your own, not just some anguished decision born of fear or guilt or uncertainty or saintliness. And we grew to be friends and admirers too, encouraging of each other's work in the world – and in those final days, daily companions who sought out each other's company. 'So many parents and children have a relationship that is grounded in some sense of duty, and it never felt thus for you and me. So, thank you, Dad, for this and more. I love you, even when you are being very stubborn, as one might think you are being now. And you knew that I loved you, and I know that you loved me. I can imagine your face, now stock-still in that coffin of yours, turning purple at such winsomeness, such sentimentality, but you were sentimental too – and there is, as you knew well, a time and a place for sentiment, and that time is now for me. Thank you, Dad. Goodbye.'

I cried a little more, and left. That was the last time I saw my father. I stepped back into the reception area of Chelsea Funeral Directors, and then out into the daylight. My brother put his arm round me, and we walked slowly back down the Fulham Road, past the old post office, and the Catholic school, and the hospital and Pizza Express – just as we might have done forty years earlier. We turned into Limerston Street, and I looked about me, and realised that I knew the location of every lamp-post and manhole cover on this street, but that the colours of the front doors had changed many times since I was a child. And then I went back into the house in which I was born.

NOTES AND SOURCES

The key sources for the first third of this book are my father's two volumes of memoirs: *Rebecca's Vest* (Hamish Hamilton, 1993), which deals largely with his first twenty-five years, and *Dark Horses* (Picador, 1998), which concentrates on his career in literary journalism. Neither of them can be described as conventional in their approach to autobiography – and they contain some of his finest writing. I've also relied heavily on my father's carefully organised collection of letters from his friends and family, including Tony White.

Many of Tony White's early letters to his friends have survived, particularly those written to John Holmstrom and Thom Gunn. Richard Murphy showed me his journal, as well as a transcription he had made in the 1990s of a journal that Tony kept sporadically.

p2 *No poor soul was ever iller*: From the final chapter of *Dark Horses*. My father follows this couplet in trochaic tetrameter with the words: 'There are days when I am my tongue, my throat, my sinus, my anus. I have house-mite's chest.' He could always laugh at his own hypochondria, and was fond of the line, ascribed to Woody Allen, 'Even hypochondriacs fall ill sometimes', and was even keener on Spike Milligan's epitaph, 'I told you I was ill'.

p4 *Rufty-Tufty*: I've recently discovered, to my consternation, that the squirrel with the unfortunate haircut was actually called Tufty Fluffytail, not Rufty-Tufty – who is in fact a golliwog in a series of children's books written by Ruth Ainsworth in the 1950s and 1960s. I can only presume that my father confused these two very different fictional characters – and put the words Rufty-Tufty into my mouth.

p4 *Leezie Lindsay*: A traditional ballad, first written down by Robert Burns, and not published until 1806, ten years after Burns' death. Several versions of the ballad exist – but they all describe the attempts of a chieftain from the Highlands to win the hand of Leezie Lindsay, a young woman who is from the south of Scotland. In all the versions I have come across, except those invented by my father, Leezie consents to head northwards when she finds out that the chieftain is very rich and powerful.

p6 *Tam O' Shanter*: In the early 1980s a new selection of poems by Burns was published (*Robert Burns*, Weidenfield and Nicholson, 1981), chosen and with an introduction by my father. The selection ends with 'Tam O' Shanter', which he describes as Burns' 'masterpiece'. The 'open presses' referred to by Burns are open cupboards.

p8 *Not Waving But Drowning*: From the anthology *Writing in England Today* (Penguin, 1968, p83) edited by Karl Miller. I grew up thinking of Stevie as a woman's name, though it's likely that a temporary teenage obsession with Stevie Nicks of Fleetwood Mac also helped me reach this conclusion.

p11 *Pentland Hills*: The Pentland Hills loomed large in the early life and writings of my father. He was born at the foot of the Pentlands, and he used to cycle there during school holidays. At the start of his first book, *Cockburn's Millennium* (Duckworth, 1975), a biography of the early nineteenth-century Scottish reformer Henry Cockburn, he declares that it is also 'a book about the beautiful and mysterious Pentland Hills'. In his will, my father said he wished to have his ashes scattered off the south coast of England, but we thought the lawyer may have just copied these instructions from my mother's will. We therefore ignored his will and scattered his ashes in the Pentlands, not far from Bonaly Tower where Cockburn lived and died. In *Cockburn's Millennium*, my father writes that 'if you stand now, on a fine day, above Bonaly... there is a sense, still, of Olympus and other heavens.'

p12 *Orphan self*: From the first volume of my father's memoirs, *Rebecca's Vest*. He named the book after a garment worn by a Jewish beauty in Sir Walter Scott's medieval romance, *Ivanhoe*. My father seems to have spent part of his teenage years fantasising about what may have lain beneath that vest.

p13 *Straight on to Penicuik*: My father goes on to describe Straiton as sitting at the foot of the 'benevolent blue Pentland Hills, from which, in wintertime, stricken deer would descend for human help, their eyes closed with ice'. Surely he made that up about the deer. He always had a soft spot for wild animals, particularly those, like deer and foxes and garden birds, who wander into urban environments.

p17 *Clapham School of Art*: In *Rebecca's Vest* my father says William studied at the Glasgow Art School. But in a letter from one of his few friends that my father received after William's death it is made clear that he actually studied in London, at the Clapham School of Art, which seems to have closed during the Second World War.

p24 *Poetry anthology*: The book was the *Oxford Book of English Verse 1250–1918*, chosen and edited by Sir Arthur Quiller-Couch (Oxford, 1939). Spencer's 'Prothalamion' is also heavily annotated, and there are long schoolboy notes on 'Kelmeny' by James Hogg. More than half a century later, my father would write a biography of Hogg (*Electric Shepherd*, Faber, 2003), in which he devoted a chapter to 'Kelmeny'.

p26 *Dylan Thomas*: Hector had sent Dylan Thomas a copy of the school magazine, *Schola Regia*, for Summer 1949, pointing out my father's two poems. Dylan Thomas was amused by what were pastiches of his style, but was not absolutely convinced that they could have been written by a schoolboy – and thought Hector might be the author.

Thomas wrote back on 15 July 1949, 'Dear Hector, thank you for the school magazine. I was sorry to see no picture of you in charge of some athletic group, but enjoyed the "Chant" and "A Group of Trees". K.M. certainly has something there, and the echoes, though I cannot place where they come from, seem to be not unpleasant. But, indeed, he might be very good. The Anonymous author of "Chant" I would, myself, take to be a far older boy with a taste for Scotch, though I may be entirely wrong.' From *The Letters of Dylan Thomas* (Paladin, 1985, p712). My father discusses this episode in *Memoirs of a Modern Scotland* (Karl Miller (ed.), Faber, 1970, pp99–101), a series of essays published in honour of Hector MacIver, four years after his death.

p33 *Wasting Fires*: The title 'Wasting Fires' was taken from *A Portrait of the Artist as a Young Man* in which Joyce refers to the 'wasting fires of lust' (Penguin, 1992, p106). My father writes at some length in *Rebecca's Vest* about *Portrait* and its influence on his teenage thoughts and guilt about sexuality.

p33 'For K.F.C.M': In *Schola Regia* (Summer 1948, p124). On re-reading this edition of the school magazine, I realise that my father wasn't yet its editor, and the poem was written about him by its then editor – so my question to him was a little unfair. There is even an announcement in the magazine that Karl Miller will be its next editor.

p35 *Nought out of twenty*: Much of the material that my father used for the chapter in *Rebecca's Vest* about his time in the army was originally published as an essay in *All Bull: The National Servicemen* (B.S. Johnson (ed.), Allison and Busby, 1973). In the essay he included an extended discussion on the similarities of being a soldier and being a footballer: 'A good soldier is likely to have the decency and calm of a good soccer professional, and one reason for this is that both men have lived in a state of subjection to unearned authority in the shape of officers and directors.'

p41 *A book about her mother*: The book is *My Improper Mother and Me* by Esther Fairfax (Pomona, 2010). Lotte Berk, née Heymansohn (1913–2003), was born in Cologne into a rich Jewish family. Her mother died while her father was telling a joke. Lotte trained as a dancer, married Ernest Berk in 1933, and fled from Nazi Germany. Her father died in Auschwitz. In the sixties, by which time my father had lost contact with her, Lotte became famous and successful as the founder of a chain of exercise studios and the inventor of the 'Lotte Berk Technique', well known for its unusually named callisthenic postures: 'The Peeing Dog', 'The French Lavatory' and 'The Prostitute'.

p41 *Smocked and sandalled love*: In *Rebecca's Vest* my father describes his poem 'as a tribute to Lotte's daughter', and it was written and published in his school magazine (*Schola Regia*, Easter 1949) prior to Lotte and my father becoming lovers. The version in *Rebecca's Vest* has just two verses, while the one in *Schola Regia* has a third verse in which my father refers to his 'bark of shining blood', and the 'throng of needles in my eye' – as a result of which he appears to lose the interest of his beloved. Esther Berk was fourteen at the time.

p47 *Charmed me off my feet*: From *My Cambridge* (Ronald Hayman (ed.), Robson Books, 1977, pp135–48). There are several other Karl Miller stories in Thom Gunn's article, including one involving a loud fart and a female professor from Newnham, and this account of my father's early method of editing poetry: 'When I wrote a new poem I would give it to him for criticism, and he would pin it to the wall above his desk for several days before he told me what he thought of it... He matured my mind amazingly, and I learned from his habit of questioning, of questioning everything.'

p57 *Priapic monolith*: From the *London Review of Books*, 26 July 1990.

p63 *World of literary magazines*: My father didn't see a great deal of difference between bringing up children and bringing out a magazine. In *Dark Horses* he writes: 'After Daniel came two other children, Sam and

Georgia. I thought of them as my three little magazines, very soon to be editing themselves.' Or maybe he was being winsome.

p71 *Almost unintelligible*: The article was by the poet and critic William Empson. In his obituary of my father (*Guardian*, 25 September 2014), John Sutherland writes that the editor of the *New Statesman*, Paul Johnson, 'as an act of goodwill, handed over a parting cheque for £3,000 – good money in 1967. Miller, as an act of independence, tore it into confetti at his editor's desk.' No one in the family had heard this story before, and we think that it is probably untrue. Paul Johnson has no recollection of it. My mother describes the months after he left the *New Statesman* as particularly difficult. They had no money and she had to borrow – and my father retreated from the world, spending a large amount of time under a blanket in his study.

p71 *Ruined The Listener*: In *Dark Horses*, my father describes how he was introduced to Auden at the Ritz Hotel. 'Auden stonily informed me: "You're the man who's ruined *The Listener*." "That's a matter of opinion," I weakly said. "Yes, it is," replied Auden: "It's *my* opinion."'

p82 *Christ figure*: From *The Kick* by Richard Murphy (*Granta*, 2002, pp3–4).

p87 *Its own quisling*: Tony's letter was written in November 1943, seven months before his brother was killed at Monte Cassino, and eight months before the Normandy landings, which were the beginning of the end of the German occupation of France. Quisling was executed at the end of the war.

p90 *Romantic-existentialist*: This and other quotations are from Thom Gunn's essay in *My Cambridge* see above note to p47.

p95 *Rash fierce blaze of riot*: From John of Gaunt's 'scepter'd isle' speech in *Richard II*, Act 2, Scene 1.

p95 *Sole imperator and Great General*: From Berowne's 'King of Codpieces' speech in *Love's Labour's Lost*, Act 3, Scene 1.

p97 *Picture Post magazine*: From *Picture Post*, 11 March 1957, pp34–5.

p98 *Leather jerkin*: A few months after I wrote this I found the leather jerkin concealed beneath a coat on a hanger in a cupboard outside my father's bedroom. It is a little worse for wear. No sign of the Glacier Mint.

p102 *Boyfriend of Sasha's*: The boyfriend and co-founder of Battersea Park F.C. was Glyn Seaborn Jones, later to find modest fame as a TV psychotherapist in the 1970s as an advocate of primal scream therapy. He had disappeared from the Battersea Park teamsheets by the early 1960s.

p104 *Soul does not clap its hands*: From the second verse of W.B. Yeats's 'Sailing to Byzantium'.

p107 *Entitled 'Elegy'*: from *Schola Regia* (Christmas 1947, p29).

p115 *Slept with C—n*: A Cambridge 'friend' of both Tony and my father. Tony, who was normally slow to anger, once struck C—n across the face, after the latter insulted Tony's girlfriend.

p119 *Suburbs of your pleasure*: From Portia's speech to her husband, Brutus, in *Julius Caesar*, Act 2, Scene 1: 'Dwell I but in the suburbs of your good pleasure.'

p123 *Bane frae bane*: William Soutar (1898–1943) died at the age of forty-five from tuberculosis. He wrote in English and Scots. The lines I've quoted mean: 'Her breasts so small and round' and 'All through the night we spoke no word / nor parted bone from bone'.

p134 *I do not recognise*: The other dancer, my mother points out, is her employer James Michie of the publishers Heinemann – who was also by this time a friend and occasional employer of Tony White.

p138 *You're the football here*: This was the first version of the story my mother told me – some fifty-two years after the event. She now believes the words 'I think you're the football here' were uttered by the abortionist Dr Gross, not the psychiatrist Dr Rolls. The relevance of this is that she went ahead and met the first of the psychologists even after the football conversation – though she says she had already made up her mind not to go ahead with the abortion. The name of the second psychiatrist, Dr Blaise-Gould, has been crossed out in her diary.

p152 *Measured his length*: From *Rebecca's Vest*. My father may have lifted this phrase from Thomas Dick Lauder's *The Wolfe of Badenoch* (Routledge, 1880), a Scottish historical romance set in the fourteenth century in which an unfortunate warhorse is knocked to the ground. See p260: 'The noble animal was so stunned by it [an axe blow], that he staggered, and measured his length on the sod.'

p152 *John Moynihan dedicated his book: Park Football* by John Moynihan (Pelham Books, 1970). For Tiny Black as an 'out-of-control Tiger tank' see p20.

p155 *Cameroonian novelist Ferdinand Oyono*: The book, *Le Vieux Nègre et la Médaille*, was published as *The Old Man and the Medal* in 1967 as part of the Heinemann African Writers Series, translated by John Reed.

p155 *Inspector Maigret stories*: The two Maigret books translated by Tony were *Maigret and the Hundred Gibbets* (Penguin, 1963) and *Maigret and the Saturday Caller* (Penguin, 1968), and he translated one of Simenon's other works – *Account Unsettled* (Penguin, 1966). I found in John Holmstrom's papers a list of all of Tony's translations: fifteen in all.

p155 *Exists in galley form*: I've tracked down a proof copy of *Words*, Tony's translation of Sartre's *Les Mots*, produced by Hamish Hamilton, and stamped on the cover with a provisional publication date of 2 July 1964. An almost identical translation by a woman called Irene Clephane, who had once worked as Siegfried Sassoon's secretary, was published later that year by Hamish Hamilton.

p156 *Nineteenth-century adventure story*: The book I translated is called, in the UK edition, *The Marvellous (But Authentic) Adventures of Captain Corcoran* (Vintage, 2016) and, in the Indian edition, *Once Upon a Time in India: the Marvellous Adventures of Captain Corcoran* (Juggernaut, 2016), written by Alfred Assollant. It was originally published as *Les Aventures Merveilleuses mais Authentiques du Capitaine Corcoran* in 1867. Sartre in *Les Mots* (see the previous note) refers to this book, something I only spotted after I had finished the translation of Corcoran. *Les Mots* is principally about the awfulness of Sartre's childhood, and he describes how *Captain Corcoran* provided him with an escape from that awfulness, almost a redemption. He writes that he read Corcoran perhaps one hundred times – and how the moment he picked up the book, even in middle age, and read its first lines, he could, in his words, 'forget myself' – *'je m'oublie'*.

p156 *The pubs of London*: The first two editions were published as the *Guide to London Pubs* by Martin Green and Tony White (Sphere, 1965, 1968) and as the *Evening Standard Guide to London Pubs* (Pan, 1973). Each edition contained a fictitious pub which readers were encouraged to identify by a process of elimination.

p156 *How to Run a Pub*: Published by Hamish Hamilton, 1969.

p156 *Contempt of Court*: Published by The Bodley Head, 1966. There are no acknowledgements, and Tony White is unmentioned in the book.

p157 *As many different jobs as possible*: The poetry tour involved organising public readings by Richard Murphy and Ted Hughes in the USA. Tony worked as a steel fixer on the construction of Seven Sisters underground station on London's Victoria Line.

p157 *Friends prosper*: Coleman is John Coleman, a film critic and poet who was at Cambridge with Tony and my father, and Holmstrom is John Holmstrom, Tony's friend from Haileybury. Both were employed by my father as critics on the *New Statesman*. Michie was James Michie (the other male dancer at the 1960 Limerston Street party – see note to p134) and the on–off employer at Heinemann of both Tony and my mother.

Wood was the theatre and TV director Peter Wood, whom Tony and my father knew at Cambridge.

p159 *Double Negative*: From *High Island* by Richard Murphy (Faber, 1974).

p163 *A subject in infant schools*: From *Writing in England Today: The Last Fifteen Years* (Penguin, 1968, p20).

p164 *The soap opera Coronation Street*: See *Writing in England Today* pp18, 20. My father too, much later, in his seventies, would become an almost uncritical fan of *Coronation Street*.

p164 *Only three names*: The other two names are of friends of my father who were also academics: John Clive and Christopher Ricks.

p164 *John Lennon is sandwiched*: Paul McCartney is stuck between Shena Mackay and John McGahern. 'Eleanor Rigby' was largely Paul's composition.

p165 *Production of King Lear*: The play was originally staged at the Nottingham Playhouse, but transferred to the Old Vic in early 1970. My parents went to see the play on 13 February 1970.

p166 *Informal company of builders*: Peter Doherty informs me that the unofficial slogan or tagline of J.N. Builders was: 'The impossible we do immediately. Miracles take a little longer.'

p170 *Met Seamus Heaney*: My father would have seen this as a tease. Seamus was a good friend of my father's and someone who had little interest in football.

p172 *Could handle a spade*: From the poem 'Digging' in Seamus Heaney's first published collection of poems, *Death of a Naturalist* (Faber, 1966). This happens to be one of the three poems by Seamus that my father published in the 4 December 1964 issue of the *New Statesman* and it was the poem which first brought him to the attention of British audiences. It was also the beginning of a friendship that lasted until Seamus died in 2013. Andrew O'Hagan has written in detail about this friendship in an introductory essay for my father's final book, *Tretower to Clyro* (Quercus, 2011). Seamus contributed a poem about my father which referred to his writings as 'passionate, precise, unobvious'. I like that.

Seated between me and the islander at the 2015 Inishbofin Literature Festival at the moment that the latter quoted 'Digging', was (unknown to the speaker) Seamus Heaney's daughter, Catherine. My father would have liked that coincidence.

p173 *Lobster pot for a chair*: This is the first verse of the poem 'Tony White at Inishbofin 1959' published in *The Price of Stone* by Richard Murphy (Faber, 1985).

p174 *I Knew the Bride by Hugo Williams*: My father wrote at length about Hugo Williams in his second volume of memoirs, *Dark Horses*.

p175 *Four days before he died*: The review appeared in *The Spectator* on 20 September 2014, more than fifty-seven years after he first wrote a review for the magazine. It contained this quotation from one of Hugo's poems, which I think he was using as a way of telling us how he felt: 'You're lucky to be alive, / but you don't see it like that. / You think you're being brave.' From the poem 'Good Thanks' in *I Knew the Bride* (Faber, 2014, p46).

p176 *Killed him almost immediately:* The official cause of death was a pulmonary embolism – which was in turn caused by 'thrombosed calf veins', an example of deep vein thrombosis, the medical name for what would later be christened 'economy class syndrome' by the media, because of occasions when the blood clot was caused by long periods of immobilisation on intercontinental flights.

p179 *My mother chose not to:* John Holmstrom did go to the mortuary, and his description of Tony makes painful reading. It took the form of an angry letter to a hospital official. 'Tony was lying with his head turned aside, and when I walked round and saw his face, I found that his eyes and mouth were still open and no attempt had been made to compose him into a normal attitude of peace. This was some 24 hours after his death – and he looked like a dead dog lying in the gutter.'

p179 *Boxed set of books:* My birthday present was *How Things Work: The Universal Encyclopaedia of Machines* (Paladin, 1977).

p180 *Richard Murphy noticed:* Richard took Tony's ashes to be both scattered and buried in Connemara, and a second wake, for his Irish friends, was held at Tony's cottage.

p182 *A master of transformations:* From the poem 'For Tony' in *Your Head in Mine* by Sasha Moorsom and Michael Young (Carcanet, 1994, p39).

p182 *Supernatural powers:* From the poem 'Tony White 1930–1976' in *The Price of Stone* by Richard Murphy (Faber, 1985).

p182 *Blessed Tony White*: From the poem 'Tony, Composite' by John Holmstrom, unpublished. The poem: 'The blessed Tony White leaned out / From the wet bar of Galway / And promised, with a blazing smile: / "I will be with you alway. / But seek no bosom-friendship now – / I left it in the hallway."'

p182 *Fantastical duke*: From the poem 'Talbot Road' in *The Passages of Joy* by Thom Gunn (Faber, 1982). Thom's previous collection *Jack Straw's Castle* (Faber, 1976) is dedicated 'to the memory of Tony White'.

p183 *Prince of panache*: I've found one more poem, 'Anniversary Ode to Battersea Park 1986', written by Martin Green, in which Tony is a lowly knight. 'There came a blow to Battersea / On its twentieth anniversary / Which brought the death of Tony White / The *fons et origo*, the knight / Whose shining armour led us all / Until that fatal leg-break fall / The game goes on, on with the game / Though we had lost our bravest name.'

p184 *Full-time professor*: My father left *The Listener* in 1973 and joined University College London as Lord Northcliffe Professor of English Literature in 1974. He didn't start working on a magazine again until 1979 when he founded the *London Review of Books*, originally as an insert in the *New York Review of Books*, and as a separate magazine in 1980. He left the *London Review of Books* in 1992.

p184 *Kept their parents busy*: My older brother kept them particularly busy at this time. He was, before and after Tony died, in the throes of a court case brought by London University (who were also my father's

employers) after he sent a friend into his French oral exam in his place –
as a little joke. He and his co-defendant were accused of conspiracy to
defraud, and the case went to trial. When the defence lawyer reminded
the court that the maximum penalty for conspiracy to defraud was thirty-
seven years, everyone laughed. The case was dismissed.

p190 *Scotland's hidden poo'ers*: Inscribed on the side of a modern cairn on
Edinburgh's Calton Hill are the words: 'For we ha'e faith in Scotland's
hidden poo'ers / The present's theirs, but a' the past and future's oors',
which are the final lines of Hugh MacDiarmid's poem 'Gairmscoile'
from his 1926 collection *Penny Wheep*.

p191 *Rob Taubman*: Alison's mother Mary had been my mother's closest
friend, the only one to whom she trusted the story of Tony White. Mary
and Rob Taubman both died in 2010.

p199 *I'm two people*: This and other quotes in this section come from *Doubles* by Karl Miller (OUP, 1985).

p203 *Stand up for bastards*: From *King Lear*, Act I, Scene 2.

p216 *I stick out wherever I go*: From *Delhi: Adventures in a Megacity*
(Jonathan Cape, 2010, p79).

ACKNOWLEDGEMENTS

This is a book that began as a funeral speech, and soon became a private investigation into the life of my father, my own life, and my immediate prehistory. It provided me with a therapy of sorts after the death of my father. Others enter psychoanalysis. Or talk to priests. Or get drunk. I write.

It only became possible to imagine publication once my mother, Jane Miller, had read the draft of the final text. We don't agree on everything – and an assiduous reader will soon see that – but she has given me her full support and encouragement in writing this book. So thanks to her, more than any other living being.

Several others have read part or all of the book in draft form, and provided me with many useful comments. These include Alexandra Pringle, Annette Ekin, Blake Morrison, Catherine Heaney, Daniel Miller, Georgia Miller, Shireen Vakil Miller and Urmila Jagannathan.

And a special thank you to Richard Murphy, without whose assistance and encouragement this would have been a lesser book. Others who have helped me, knowingly or not, include Peter Doherty, Tom Paine, Clare Moynihan, Emily Murphy, Esther Fairfax, Katie Forman, Sue Preston, the late Lois Preston, Margaret Day, Ann Day, Kieran Day, Ardashir

Vakil, Rahul Noble Singh, Catherine Goodman, Roxane Delgado, Laurent Binet, Eloise Carbert, Fiona Green, Katie Green, Esther Freud, Elston Gunn, Mike Kitay, Andrew O'Hagan, Brienne of Tarth, Ferzina Banaji, Penelope Wilton, Alison Bechdel, Jonathan and Rachel Miller, Margie Owen, Steven Sackur, Penny Richards, Chloe Paidoussis, Karuna Nundy, Christabel McEwen, Josh Ritter, Lizzie Goodfriend, Tony Scotland, Sophie Young, Andrew Whitehead, Hugo Williams, Alison Taubman, Erwan Fouéré, Olwen Fouéré and my former colleagues in the BBC Media Action offices in Nigeria and Tunisia.

Thank you also to those most directly involved in the publication of the book by Jonathan Cape: Dan Franklin, Ana Fletcher, Rachel Cugnoni, Michal Shavit, Neil Bradford and Suzanne Dean. Many thanks to my agent David Godwin.

This book is dedicated to my parents, all two-and-a-half of them – but it is also very much a book for my own children, Zubin and Roxana. They loved my father, Karl Miller, who loved them back – and it pleases me greatly that they grew to know him as young adults. It was a tradition of mine to blame these aforementioned children for any errors in my writings, since they were once sharers of my computer, but they have now flown the coop, and anyway have far fancier devices of their own these days. So I have to take full responsibility for any mistakes. However, I have, in maintenance of another tradition, deliberately inserted a small error as a little joke. If you are the first to spot it – tell me, you will be awarded appropriately.

INDEX

The author and publishers gratefully acknowledge permission given to reprint material from the following copyright holders:

The Estate of James MacGibbon for permission to quote from Stevie Smith's poem 'Not Waving But Drowning'.

Richard Murphy for permission to quote from his poems, memoirs and private journals.

Hugo Williams for permission to quote from his poem 'Good Thanks'.

The Estate of Sasha Moorsom for permission to quote from the poem 'For Tony'.

The Estate of John Holmstrom for permission to quote from an unpublished poem about Tony White.

The Estate of Seamus Heaney for permission to quote from the poem 'Digging'.

The Estate of Martin Green for permission to quote from an unpublished poem about Battersea Park football team.

Katie Green for permission to use a photo of her with Tony White.

The Estate of Thom Gunn for permission to quote from the poem 'Talbot Road'.